THE ANXIOUS GENERATION GOES TO CHURCH

What the Research Says
about What Younger Generations
Need (and Want) from Your Church

The Anxious Generation Goes to Church

Thom S. Rainer

TYNDALE
MOMENTUM®

A Tyndale nonfiction imprint

Visit Tyndale Momentum online at tyndalemomentum.com.

Tyndale, Tyndale's quill logo, *Tyndale Momentum*, and the Tyndale Momentum logo are registered trademarks of Tyndale House Ministries. Tyndale Momentum is a nonfiction imprint of Tyndale House Publishers, Carol Stream, Illinois.

The Anxious Generation Goes to Church: What the Research Says about What Younger Generations Need (and Want) from Your Church

Cover designed by Eva M. Winters

Interior designed by Laura Cruise

Some names have been changed to protect the privacy of individuals.

For information about special discounts for bulk purchases, please contact Tyndale House Publishers at csresponse@tyndale.com, or call 1-855-277-9400.

Library of Congress Cataloging-in-Publication Data

A catalog record for this book is available from the Library of Congress.

ISBN 978-1-4964-4922-1

Printed in the United States of America

31 30 29 28 27 26 25
7 6 5 4 3 2 1

To Nathaniel Rainer.

You are a leader and missionary to your generation.

I love you.

I'm proud of you.

I thank God that you are my grandson.

And always to Nellie Jo.

Your smile captured my life.

Your love captured my heart.

Contents

Foreword

WHEN I BEGAN TAKING COURSES toward a doctoral degree in 2005, the most famous scholar of political science was Harvard professor Dr. Robert Putnam. The book that led to his initial fame was called *Making Democracy Work*, which explored why most regional governments were thriving in northern Italy, while those in the southern part of the country were struggling. His answer was that those in the northern regions had strong civic organizations and cooperative societies, which were lacking in other parts of the country. Putnam later brought that simple idea—that social connection could lead to all kinds of societal improvements—to the mainstream in his magnum opus, *Bowling Alone: The Collapse and Revival of American Community*. What Putnam found, through collecting heaps of data, was that Americans were abandoning all the civic organizations that had helped bind communities together. They were no longer joining the Elks, the American Legion, the Boy Scouts, or bowling leagues. Why was this happening? Well, among other possible contributors to the "shrinking stock of social capital"[1] in American society, Putnam identified the explosive growth of cable television.

Though cable was all the rage in the late 1990s when Putnam was writing *Bowling Alone*, he couldn't possibly have predicted what the next two decades would bring—the nearly universal adoption of home internet, the invention of the smartphone, and the absolutely transformative power of social media. Social science is just beginning to wrap its arms around all the implications of the huge shift that happened at such a rapid pace. That's why Jonathan Haidt's *The Anxious Generation* was such an important addition to this literature. For the first time, a respected social scientist collected and synthesized hundreds of studies that all arrived at the same conclusion: The information age was having profound negative effects on the social and psychological lives of young people.

To this point, churches have largely remained on the fringes of this issue, assuming the role of slightly concerned observers. Every once in a while a pastor will ask me what impact I think smartphones and social media are having on the young people who are occupying their pews with less and less frequency every year. In *The Anxious Generation Goes to Church*, Thom Rainer provides a helpful way for Christians to think through the implications of the technological age. With clarity and practicality, Thom points to some of the significant differences between this generation of young people and those who came before. It is empirically true that Generation Z is the safest cohort (physically) in our nation's history. They were watched like hawks by their parents if they tried to ride their bicycles beyond the end of the driveway. At the same time, they are moving into adulthood much more slowly than those from a generation or two ago. The share of high school students who are smoking cigarettes or drinking alcohol is a fraction of what it was thirty years ago. But also the share who are working part-time jobs, getting their driver's license, and finding a romantic partner is dramatically lower than was true of the Millennials at the same age. What changed for those born in the 1980s compared to those born in the early 2000s? The only answer that makes any sense is the rise of smartphones, which became ubiquitous around the time that Gen Zers were entering their vulnerable adolescent years.

It's time for churches to take more than a passive bystander approach to this growing problem of social alienation. What I so much appreciate about Thom Rainer's approach in this book is that he doesn't oversell the role that churches can play in solving this emerging crisis. That's a point that cannot be emphasized enough: The American church is not some type of panacea for all the ills facing the United States. But it certainly should be more proactive in trying to alleviate the anxiety, depression, and loneliness that a growing number of Americans are facing.

The famed American investor and philanthropist Warren Buffett is fond of saying, "You don't find out who's been swimming naked until the tide goes out."[2] As American religion has ebbed over the last three decades, the true vulnerabilities of the church have been laid bare. Hundreds of books have been written on hypocrisy and corruption in religious institutions. But what also has been revealed is the real value that religion plays in a functioning society. The idea that animated Putnam's research is so simple and yet so profound: *Social connection matters*. When those ties begin to fray, it leads to all kinds of problems. I think we are discovering that now as a society. The tide has receded and a lot of the dysfunction in American culture has been made plain to us. The American church stands as one of the last major generators of social capital. Religious leaders should take heed that the role of their houses of worship extends far beyond helping people find connection with God. It can also help congregants build strong ties with people around them. That's especially the case among young people, who are more technologically connected but more socially isolated than ever. What's at stake is not just the future of American religion, but the future of the American experiment. It's time for the church to lead.

RYAN P. BURGE
Associate professor of political science, Eastern Illinois University
Author of *The Nones*

Introduction

Coming to Grips with the Anxious Generation

I WAS WELL ON MY WAY to completing the research on a different book when I hit a wall. I wasn't entirely settled on the concept, and I found myself staring at a blank computer screen—the bane of every writer's existence—for just a little too long one morning.

I've written enough books to know that sometimes you just have to push through and start writing, even if you're not feeling it that day; but on this particular morning, pushing through didn't seem like it would be at all productive. I figured I wouldn't lose my momentum if I gave the project another twenty-four hours to percolate, so I set it aside.

That afternoon, a book I had ordered arrived—*The Anxious Generation* by Jonathan Haidt. It was at the top of the bestsellers list, and I was intrigued by the title, but it was the subtitle that had really caught my eye: *How the Great Rewiring of Childhood Is Causing an Epidemic of Mental Illness.*

I try to keep up with significant cultural developments, and *The Anxious Generation* seemed to fit the bill. When I read the description of the book before ordering and discovered it was about an epidemic of anxiety, depression, and mental illness in my grandchildren's generations—Gen Z (born between 1997 and 2012) and Gen Alpha (born since 2013)—my interest quickly became personal. I realized, *This directly affects my kids, my grandkids, and all their friends.*

If you've read my other books or ever heard me speak, you know how much I love my family. That love has grown dramatically with the addition of eleven grandchildren. Of the ten who are still living (sadly, we lost Will Rainer an hour after his birth in 2011), five are Gen Z and five are Gen Alpha. So "the great rewiring" refers to both their generations.

I started reading at ten o'clock that night, and I couldn't put the book down. After pausing for a nap around four in the morning, I resumed my reading a few hours later. Around noon, I called Jon Farrar, my publisher at Tyndale House, and told him about *The Anxious Generation*. I was beginning to realize that it was foundational for something that had been on my mind for a while—namely, how does the church reach Gen Z? Fewer members of that generation are Christians than any other living generation, and even fewer attend church on a regular basis. Jonathan Haidt's book provides a wealth of information about the struggles of the younger generations, and I was confident that I could build on his findings and offer some ideas for how the local church can reach Gen Z.

Jon asked for a day or so to look at the concept. When he shared it with his team at Tyndale House, their enthusiasm matched mine, which is always a good way to start a new book project.

But even after *The Anxious Generation Goes to Church* was given the green light, I knew it would be a long journey to publication. Frankly, if I had known how many hours I would spend researching for this book, my excitement undoubtedly would not have been as great. But sometimes ignorance is bliss. Now that everything is done, I know it was the book I needed to write.

What Is the Anxious Generation?

The "Anxious Generation" refers to unforeseen consequences of what happened in the culture at large, and to Gen Z in particular, as a result of two societal trends that converged between 2010 and 2015, just as Gen Z was starting to come of age.

The first trend was what Jonathan Haidt calls "the rise of fearful and overprotective parenting."[1] This actually began in the 1980s, when parents became increasingly concerned about their children's safety out in the world and started curtailing their freedom to roam and play unsupervised—a core freedom that the parents themselves had enjoyed as products of an earlier age. I know about this shift from firsthand experience.

Nellie Jo and I, with our young family, were living in Louisville, Kentucky, in 1983, just a few miles from where a twelve-year-old girl named Ann Gotlib disappeared while riding her bike in an area that was perceived to be safe. Her disappearance, and other high-profile kidnapping cases around the same time, ushered in a new era and awareness as the national spotlight focused on missing children.[2] Ann Gotlib was never found.

My sons were born in 1980, 1982, and 1985. When they were old enough to start riding bikes, Nellie Jo and I refused to let them out of our sight while they rode. And even as they got older, we didn't allow them to ride their bikes in the neighborhood without clear boundaries. The world just didn't feel as safe as it once had.

The second trend was the emergence of digital technology, and more specifically the combination of high-speed internet, smartphones, and viral social media. As Haidt describes it,

> These products made life easier, more fun, and more productive. Some of them helped people to connect and communicate, and . . . it felt like the dawn of a new age. . . .
>
> But the tech industry wasn't just transforming life for adults. It began transforming life for children too. . . . The new technologies were far more portable,

> personalized, and engaging than anything that came before. . . . Many parents were relieved to find that a smartphone or tablet could keep a child happily engaged and quiet for hours. Was this safe? Nobody knew, but because everyone else was doing it, everyone just assumed that it must be okay.
>
> Yet the companies had done little or no research on the mental health effects of their products on children and adolescents. . . . They hooked children during vulnerable developmental stages, while their brains were rapidly rewiring in response to incoming stimulation. This included social media companies, which inflicted their greatest damage on girls, and video game companies and pornography sites, which sank their hooks deepest into boys. By designing a firehose of addictive content that entered through kids' eyes and ears, and by displacing physical play and in-person socializing, these companies have rewired childhood and changed human development on an almost unimaginable scale.[3]

Of greatest concern to Haidt and others is that "when adolescents' social lives moved onto smartphones and social media platforms, anxiety and depression surged among them."[4] As Haidt summarizes his thesis, "Two trends—*overprotection in the real world and underprotection in the virtual world*—are the major reasons why children born after 1995 became the anxious generation."[5] Psychologist Jean Twenge, in her book *Generations*, adds, "Social media changed the lives of people of all ages after it became popular after 2010, but it had a bigger impact on younger people since they were still building their social lives and communication skills. Although older people began to use social media, too, they had already developed their social ties and honed their communication skills in an earlier, less technology-saturated time."[6]

The Great Rewiring

In *The Anxious Generation*, Jonathan Haidt explores how the constant influx of information, much of it negative or misleading, fundamentally changes the way older children and adolescents think and feel. He calls this "the great rewiring." The great rewiring is not just about the information young people receive but also how their brains process and respond to it.

Haidt argues that the pervasive use of social media rewires the adolescent brain to seek instant gratification and validation. Likes, shares, and comments become measures of self-worth, leading to a perpetual cycle of seeking approval from others.

This external validation can create a fragile sense of self, heavily dependent on the opinions of peers and strangers alike. The problem is exacerbated by the curated nature of social media, where people present idealized versions of their lives. This leads to constant comparisons, making young people feel inadequate and anxious.

The impact of this rewiring is profound. It affects not only individual mental health but also social dynamics and relationships. Haidt notes that the rise in anxiety and depression among Gen Z coincided with the widespread adoption of smartphones and social media.

This is not merely a coincidence; it's a clear indication of how technology influences mental health. The brain, constantly bombarded with notifications and updates, rarely finds time to rest and reflect. This constant stimulation can lead to burnout and an inability to cope with the challenges of daily life.

One of the most concerning aspects of the great rewiring is its impact on empathy and social skills. Haidt explains that meaningful face-to-face interactions are essential for developing empathy. However, as communication moves increasingly online, these embodied interactions diminish. Social media interactions often lack the depth and emotional nuance of real-life conversations, leading to superficial relationships and a decreased ability to empathize with others.

Haidt also highlights the role of algorithms in this rewiring process. Social media platforms use algorithms to keep users engaged, often promoting content that elicits strong emotional reactions. This can create echo chambers where users are exposed only to information that reinforces their existing beliefs, further polarizing society. The algorithms prioritize sensationalism and outrage, contributing to a more anxious and divided generation.

How Will the Church Respond?

My purpose here is not to dissect the details of how the Anxious Generation came to be, or what has become of them. Jonathan Haidt does a more than adequate job of that, and you can read his book to find out more. My concern is how the local church will respond to an Anxious Generation that came of age in a culture of disembodied, asynchronous communication[†] and virtual, uncommitted, short-lived, and often disposable relationships.[7] As Haidt observes,

> Gen Z became the first generation in history to
> go through puberty with a portal in their pockets
> that called them away from the people nearby
> and into an alternative universe that was exciting,
> addictive, unstable, and . . . unsuitable for children

[†] Unlike synchronous communication (such as phone calls or face-to-face conversations) that happens at the same time, asynchronous communication (such as texting and emailing) occurs independently—that is, not at the same time or speed, and responses can be delayed.

> and adolescents. . . . They spent far less time playing with, talking to, touching, or even making eye contact with their friends and families, thereby reducing their participation in embodied social behaviors that are essential for successful human development. . . . It's as if they became the first generation to grow up on Mars.[8]

This trend is likely to get worse with the rise of artificial intelligence and further disembodiment of the human experience. I believe the answer lies, in part, in creating a climate in which church participation is embodied, synchronous, within a stable group setting, where "people are strongly motivated to invest in relationships and repair rifts when they happen."[9]

The challenge we face in the local church over the next decade is how to *attract*, *assimilate*, and *retain* the anxious members of Gen Z, Gen Alpha, and whatever generation comes next. This is the vital question that we Boomers, Xers, and Millennials must answer for the good of the body of Christ—and by extension, for society at large. The sea change wrought by the proliferation of digital technologies affects all of us to varying degrees, but most decidedly Gen Z and Gen Alpha—those who have grown up (or are growing up) fully immersed.

The older members of Gen Alpha are now moving into adolescence—those critical years when the convergence of smartphone technology and social media are the most disruptive to social development, self-image, and mental health. So while my primary focus is on Gen Z—the first generation to grow up as digital natives and who are now moving into the phase of life where they are making decisions about marriage, family, and church—much of what I will discuss applies to Gen Alpha as well.

As the Anxious Generation now rears the next generation, while still fully immersed in everything that made them the Anxious

Generation in the first place, the church must be prepared to reach them and teach them, love them and support them as they navigate an increasingly complex and challenging cultural landscape. After all, they are the future of the church.

A Surprising Lack of Urgency

I've learned that when writing a book based on research, it rarely follows the original outline. Such was the case with *The Anxious Generation Goes to Church*. The research shaped the book in ways that surprised me.

For example, I initially thought the book would be primarily for youth pastors and children's leaders in churches. But I realized pretty quickly that the issues and answers have a broader application to the local church as a whole.

I thought I would find a lot of urgency in churches about reaching Gen Z and Gen Alpha. But I wasn't expecting to find a more significant sense of urgency in the non-Christian world than in American churches. Atheists and agnostics often recognize the value of religious institutions more than churches themselves do. So I have devoted an entire chapter to a discussion of how the irreligious world is imploring the church to get its act together.

The non-Christian world views the church, and other religious institutions, as beneficial for many temporal needs, including relieving anxiety and depression, and giving people a sense of hope and purpose. Churches should have that same perspective—plus an eternal perspective as well. We Christians and churchgoers believe that Christ has the answer for our lives today, but we also believe he is the only answer for our eternity.

Where, then, is the evangelistic urgency in our churches?

I don't pull any punches when describing the challenges we face in the church. But if our congregations will begin to take seriously the importance of reaching and helping the Anxious Generation, I believe we will see hope and vision emerge as well.

Many in the Anxious Generation are struggling. But we in the church have a miraculous message of transformation for them.

As I write this book, I am keenly aware that its readership might include some parents who are not Christians. I know many young adults who care deeply about their children but are not followers of Christ. If you are among those who fit this description, I welcome you. It's likely you picked up this book because you want to know if the local church is a place that can help your kids and your family. I believe it can.

My central thesis is that the church might be the best place for your family—particularly your children—to find real-life community, support, and encouragement. I pray you will discover that the church can make a big difference in your children's mental and emotional health. Even more important, I am convinced that the true solution to our challenges in life is a living relationship with Jesus Christ. The church as an organization can certainly help, but it is Jesus himself who is the source of all healing, both physical and spiritual, temporal and eternal.

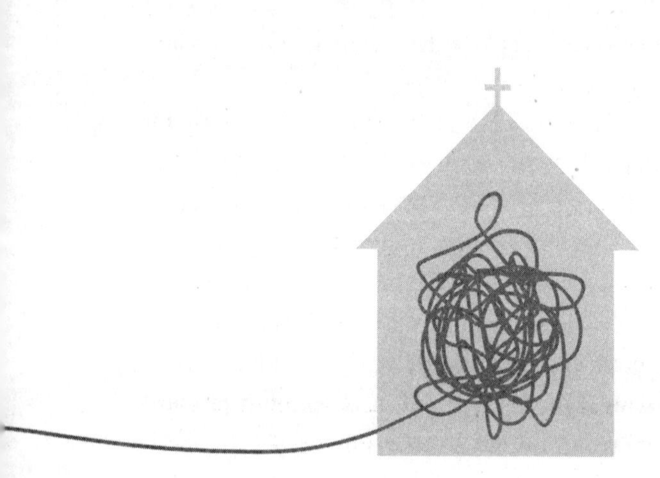

1
GENERATION GAPS

MY GENERATION, known as the Baby Boomers, or simply Boomers, was the first generation in human history subjected to massive levels of targeted research and marketing. Volumes of information have been produced in books, papers, presentations, conferences, and courses. Though we can debate the reasons behind the fascination, the primary motivation was simply a matter of pragmatism. A lot of babies were born between 1946 and 1964, and sellers of goods and services wanted to reach the families of the Boomers. To put it bluntly, it was good for business.

After the Second World War, the nation experienced an unprecedented population boom. There were 76 million live births in the US between 1946 and 1964, the years that delineate the Boomer generation.[1] The post–World War II euphoria introduced economic prosperity as soldiers returning from the war earned college degrees using the GI Bill, settled into new homes, and started new businesses made affordable by government-subsidized financing. Couples not only wanted families, they also wanted big families. There was a sustained sense of optimism that our country had not previously experienced.

The study and marketing of the Boomers birthed an entire industry of generational research. Each subsequent generation has been labeled, researched, scrutinized, theorized, and marketed. I've written two generational books myself, *The Bridger Generation* and *The Millennials* (with Jess Rainer).

Apart from the population explosion that inaugurated the Boomer generation, the boundaries of the other generations are less certain, with plenty of overlap. Researchers tend to look at changes in the number of live births, distinct cultural events (such as the Great Depression, World War II, the Vietnam War, the Kennedy/King assassinations, 9/11), economic influences, and technological advances. Of those factors, technology has emerged as the primary driver of generational differences. What distinguishes Gen Z in particular is the intersection of major technological changes (internet, smartphone, social media) with the most formative years of that generation's physical and social development.

In *The Anxious Generation*, Jonathan Haidt is not as concerned with generational markers as he is with understanding the reasons behind the challenges facing Gen Z in particular. In fact, Haidt is not ready to put an end date on the Anxious Generation until it becomes clear that the conditions that made them anxious have substantially been addressed.

That said, and without getting into the rationale for the dates I've chosen, the following chart shows the birthdate parameters I'm using for each generation, dating back to 1928, the year before the beginning of the Great Depression.

GENERATIONS IN THE UNITED STATES

Generation	Birth Years	Number of Live Births (millions)
The Silent Generation	1928–1945	52
Baby Boomers	1946–1964	76
Gen X	1965–1979	55
Millennials (Gen Y)	1980–1996	72
Gen Z (the Anxious Generation)	1997–2012	69
Gen Alpha	2013–present	(ongoing)

Sources: US Census Bureau; US Centers for Disease Control and Prevention: National Center for Health Statistics; Statistical Abstract of the United States, and USAFacts.

Let's look a bit closer at each generation. The better we understand our history, the more clearly we can see our present.

The Silent Generation (1928–1945)

The Silent Generation is often characterized by its resilience, discipline, and strong sense of duty. This generation grew up in a period marked by significant economic hardship, global conflict, and societal transformation. Their formative years were shaped by the Great Depression and World War II, which profoundly influenced their values, work ethic, and worldview.

Resilience in Hard Times

The Silent Generation experienced the Great Depression firsthand. This economic catastrophe taught them the importance of frugality, hard work, and perseverance. Many members of this generation grew up in households where financial stability was uncertain and luxuries were few. This early exposure to hardship instilled a deep-seated sense of resourcefulness and resilience that would carry them through their adult lives.

World War II and After

World War II played a crucial role in shaping the Silent Generation. Many of them served in the military or supported the war effort on the home front. The war fostered a strong sense of patriotism and collective responsibility. The post-war period brought economic prosperity, but it also reinforced traditional gender roles, with men returning to the workforce and women often returning to domestic roles.

A Focus on Stability and Security

The Silent Generation sought stability and security in the wake of the war. They valued steady employment, homeownership, and raising families in safe environments. This pursuit of stability often led them to prioritize long-term jobs with a single employer, contributing to the growth of corporate America and the development of the suburban lifestyle.

Contributions to Culture and Society

The Silent Generation's legacy is one of steadfastness and quiet determination. They were instrumental in building modern America, contributing to its economic, cultural, and social foundations. Their experiences and values affected subsequent generations, shaping how we view work, family, and civic duty.

Despite being labeled as "silent," this generation made significant cultural and societal contributions. They played a pivotal role in the civil rights movement, laying the groundwork for the social changes that would follow in the 1960s. Icons like Martin Luther

King Jr. emerged from this generation, advocating for justice and equality.

Five Key Influences

The Great Depression: Instilled values of frugality, resourcefulness, and perseverance.
World War II: Fostered patriotism, collective responsibility, and traditional gender roles.
Economic Stability: Prioritized steady employment, homeownership, and family security.
Civil Rights Movement: Played a significant role in advocating social justice and equality.
Cultural Contributions: Influenced American culture through music, literature, and social movements.

The Baby Boomers (1946–1964)

The Baby Boomer generation represents a significant demographic shift in American history. Following World War II, the United States experienced an unprecedented birth rate surge, giving rise to this influential generation. The Baby Boomers have been a driving force in shaping the modern world's social, cultural, and economic landscape.

Post-War Prosperity and Growth

The Baby Boomers grew up during a time of significant economic growth and prosperity. The post-war boom led to the creation of numerous job opportunities, suburban expansion, and a rise in consumerism. This generation benefitted from unprecedented access to education, with the GI Bill enabling many to attend college and secure better-paying jobs. This economic stability allowed

Baby Boomers to enjoy a higher standard of living than their predecessors.

Cultural Revolution

The 1960s and 1970s were transformative decades for the Baby Boomers. This period saw a cultural revolution characterized by significant shifts in music, fashion, and social norms.

The civil rights movement, the feminist movement, and antiwar protests marked this era. Baby Boomers played a critical role in challenging the status quo, advocating for social justice, gender equality, and peace. This cultural upheaval led to greater individualism and a break from traditional values.

Technological Advancements

As the Baby Boomers entered adulthood, they witnessed and contributed to significant technological advancements. The space race, culminating in the moon landing in 1969, ignited a passion for science and technology. Later, the advent of personal computers and the internet revolutionized the way people work, communicate, and access information. Baby Boomers were at the forefront of these innovations, driving technological progress and adapting to new ways of living and working.

Economic Impact

The Baby Boomers' entry into the workforce had a substantial economic impact. They fueled economic growth through their consumer habits, investment in real estate, and entrepreneurial ventures.

This generation has accumulated significant wealth, influencing market trends and shaping the economy. However, as they retire, concerns about the strain on Social Security and healthcare systems have emerged, highlighting the long-term impact of an aging population.

Legacy and Influence

The Baby Boomers' legacy is marked by their contributions to societal change, economic growth, and technological progress. Their quest for personal fulfillment, coupled with their drive for social justice, left a lasting impact on subsequent generations. As they continue to age, their influence remains evident in many aspects of modern life.

Five Key Influences

Post-War Economic Prosperity: Benefitted from economic growth, job opportunities, and increased access to education.

Cultural Revolution: Played a pivotal role in the civil rights movement, feminist movement, and anti-war protests, leading to significant societal changes.

Technological Advancements: Witnessed and contributed to major technological progress, including the space race and the rise of digital technology.

Economic Impact: Influenced market trends through consumer habits, real estate investment, and entrepreneurship.

Legacy of Social Change: Advocated for social justice, gender equality, and individualism, leaving a lasting impact on modern society.

Generation X (1965–1979)

Gen X is a pivotal cohort, bridging between the expansive Baby Boomers and the technologically savvy Millennials. Often described as the "middle child" of generations, Gen Xers experienced a unique blend of cultural, social, and technological transitions that profoundly shaped their identity.

Economic Uncertainty

Gen Xers grew up during a time of significant change. They witnessed the end of the Cold War, the rise of personal computing, and the advent of the internet. Unlike their Boomer predecessors, who enjoyed post-war optimism and economic prosperity, Gen Xers faced economic instability during their formative years. The oil crisis, high unemployment rates, and inflation of the 1970s and 1980s contributed to a sense of skepticism and resilience among this generation.

The Digital Revolution

Education and media played critical roles in shaping Gen X. The introduction of personal computers into homes and schools marked a turning point, providing Gen Xers with firsthand experience of the digital revolution. This generation also saw the birth of cable television and the MTV era, influencing their tastes in music, fashion, and entertainment. Pop culture phenomena such as the rise of hip-hop, grunge music, and iconic movies like the *Star Wars* franchise, *Fast Times at Ridgemont High*, and *The Breakfast Club* left an indelible mark on their collective consciousness.

Social Change

Socially, Gen Xers are known for their independence and self-reliance. Growing up during an era of increasing divorce rates and the rise of dual-income families, many Gen Xers became latchkey kids, learning to navigate the world with less direct supervision than previous generations. This independence fostered a sense of autonomy and adaptability that would later define their approach to work and family life.

Work and Home

Gen Xers have been recognized in the workplace for their entrepreneurial spirit and pragmatic outlook. They entered the job market during the technological boom of the 1990s, capitalizing on new opportunities in various industries. Despite facing economic recessions, Gen Xers have demonstrated resilience and flexibility, often balancing traditional work values with a desire for work-life balance.

As parents, Gen Xers have influenced their children, Generation Z and Generation Alpha, by emphasizing the importance of education, technological proficiency, and critical thinking. They have fostered environments that encourage creativity and adaptability, preparing their offspring for a rapidly changing world.

Five Key Influences

Economic Instability: Developed both skepticism and resilience as they experienced the oil crisis, inflation, and high unemployment rates of the 1970s and 1980s.

Technological Revolution: Were strongly shaped by the rise of personal computing and the internet.

Cultural Shifts: Share collective cultural memories from the influence of cable TV, MTV, and pop culture phenomena such as hip-hop and grunge music.

Social Dynamics: Became more independent and adaptable through their experience as latchkey kids as divorce rates and dual-income families increased.

Workplace Evolution: Developed an entrepreneurial spirit and adapted to technological advancements in the job market.

Millennials (1980–1996)

As the first generation to come of age in the new millennium, Millennials have been profoundly shaped by rapid technological advancements, globalization, and shifting social norms. This generation is often described as tech-savvy, diverse, and socially conscious, with experiences that have set them apart from previous generations. Though while they were growing up they did not have access to the portable digital devices that are pervasive today, Millennials were introduced to a plethora of games that held their eyes and attention. They are not the Anxious Generation, but there were signs pointing in that direction. Indeed, the Millennials would become the parents of the Anxious Generation.

The First Digital Natives

Growing up during the rise of the internet and the proliferation of digital technology, Millennials are true digital natives. They experienced the transition from dial-up modems to high-speed internet, from bulky desktop computers to sleek smartphones, and from traditional media to social media. Constant connectivity has influenced their communication styles, making them adept at using various digital platforms to build relationships, share information, and mobilize for social causes.

Degrees, Debt, and Delays

Education played a pivotal role in shaping the Millennial generation. With increased access to information and learning tools, Millennials are among the most educated generations. They have been encouraged to pursue higher education, often resulting in significant student loan debt. This financial burden has affected their life choices, including delaying significant milestones such as buying a home or starting a family.

Economic Challenges

Economically, Millennials have faced unique challenges. Entering the workforce during the Great Recession of 2008, many Millennials struggled with unemployment or underemployment, leading to a more cautious financial outlook. However, this generation is also characterized by their entrepreneurial spirit, with many turning to gig economy jobs, freelancing, and startup ventures as alternative career paths.

Diversity, Equity, and Inclusion

Socially, Millennials are known for their emphasis on diversity, equity, and inclusion. They have championed causes related to gender equality, LGBTQ+ rights, and racial justice. Even as the value of DEI is now questioned by a large segment of the population, Millennials are still known to advocate for many of its values. Growing up in a more multicultural society has made them more open to different perspectives and more committed to social change.

Workplace and Marketplace

In the workplace, Millennials seek purpose and fulfillment over traditional markers of success. They value work-life balance, flexible work arrangements, and opportunities for professional growth. Employers have had to adapt to these preferences by offering more dynamic and inclusive work environments.

Millennials have also been influential as consumers, driving the rise of the experience economy. They prioritize experiences over material possessions, favoring travel, dining, and entertainment. This shift has led to changes in various industries, from hospitality to retail.

Five Key Influences

Technological Advancements: Are true digital natives, having grown up with the rise of the internet, social media, and smartphones.

Education and Student Debt: Have increased access to higher education and the associated financial burdens.

Economic Challenge: Entered the workforce during the Great Recession and adapted to the gig economy.

Social Consciousness: Advocate for diversity, inclusion, and social justice.

Consumer Preferences: Value experiences over material possessions, affecting various industries.

Generation Z (1997–2012)

Gen Z is the first generation "to spend their entire adolescence in the age of the smartphone,"[2] internet, and social media. In the words of one observer, "Today's super-connected kids are growing up less rebellious, more tolerant, less happy—and completely unprepared for adulthood."[3]

Defined by Diversity and Individualism

"Gen Z is the most racially and ethnically diverse generation of American adults to date. . . . There are more multiracial Gen Zers than in any previous generation. Gen Z will likely be the last generation where any one racial group is in the majority in the United States."[4] Gen Z is also characterized by an increasing fluidity in the concepts of gender and sexual orientation, including widespread acceptance of bisexual and transgender identities. According to Jean Twenge, "Overall, 8.6 percent of young adults born between 2003 and 2006 (now ages 18 to 21) identify as nonbinary, compared to

6.0 percent of those born 1995–1999 (ages 25 to 29) and 7.5 percent of those born 2000–2002 (ages 22 to 24). Most strikingly, 10.6 percent of those born female from 2003 to 2006 identify as nonbinary. That's nearly 1 out of 9."[5] While the speed at which societal perspectives have changed is somewhat alarming, there is a certain logical consistency to it. "If people are all unique individuals, then it follows that gender identity is an individual choice."[6]

Growing Up Slowly

Gen Z teens are much less likely than teens from earlier generations to have a driver's license, have dated or had sex, drink alcohol, or work for pay—all indicators of a delayed or postponed independence and preparation for adulthood.[7] As psychologist Jean Twenge observes, "These trends are not all bad or good. They are not an indicator of teens being more responsible or less responsible, or more mature or less mature, but simply of teens taking their time to grow up."[8]

Slower to Marry and (Maybe) Have Children

As this book goes to press in early 2025, the eldest members of Gen Z are reaching their late twenties, a time when most earlier generations were already married and starting their families. But whereas in 1960, close to 70 percent of women in their early twenties were married (and nearly half the men), by 2020 those numbers had dropped to one in ten for women and only one in fourteen for men.[9] And according to Jean Twenge, "There are some early signs that Gen Z might not just postpone marriage and relationships, but not enter them at all."[10]

Loneliness, Depression, and Suicide on the Rise

As Jonathan Haidt describes in *The Anxious Generation*, when smartphone technology put the internet and social media in the palm of everyone's hand, the generation most adversely affected was the one just entering the most formative years of late childhood, adolescence, and early adulthood—that is, Gen Z. The adverse effects of replacing the play-based childhood familiar to Boomers and Gen Xers with an increasingly phone-based, online childhood—with a sharp reduction in in-person, embodied social interaction—resulted in alarming increases in loneliness, anxiety, depression, and suicide among members of Gen Z.

Five Key Influences

Technological Immersion: Are the first generation with no memory of a time before high-speed internet, smartphones, and viral social media.

Growing Up Slowly: Postponing or forgoing teenage rites of passage, marriage, and family.

Diversity and Tolerance: Adopting fluid gender and sexuality norms, tolerant of individual choice but not necessarily differing viewpoints.

Isolation and Virtual Relationships: Experience less emphasis on embodied interactions, greater loneliness, anxiety, and loss of community. Emergence of the social validation feedback loop of social media (likes, followers, retweets, comments).

Income Insecurity: Have less sense of opportunity, likely not to match their parents' standard of living.

The Declining Birth Rate

The birth rate in the United States has declined steadily since its peak during the Baby Boomer generation.[11] This trend results from a complex interplay of economic, social, cultural, and technological factors.

Economic uncertainty has likely played a significant role in the declining birth rate as well. The 2008 financial crisis left many young adults facing financial insecurity. High levels of unemployment and underemployment have made couples hesitant to start families.

Additionally, the increasing cost of living, particularly for housing, health care, food, and education, has made raising children more expensive, leading many to delay having children due to financial constraints. Rising student loan debt has also financially burdened many young adults, causing them to postpone marriage and childbearing.

Social and cultural shifts have also contributed to the decline in birth rates. Societal attitudes toward marriage and family have changed significantly, with less social pressure to marry and have children. There is greater acceptance of diverse family structures.

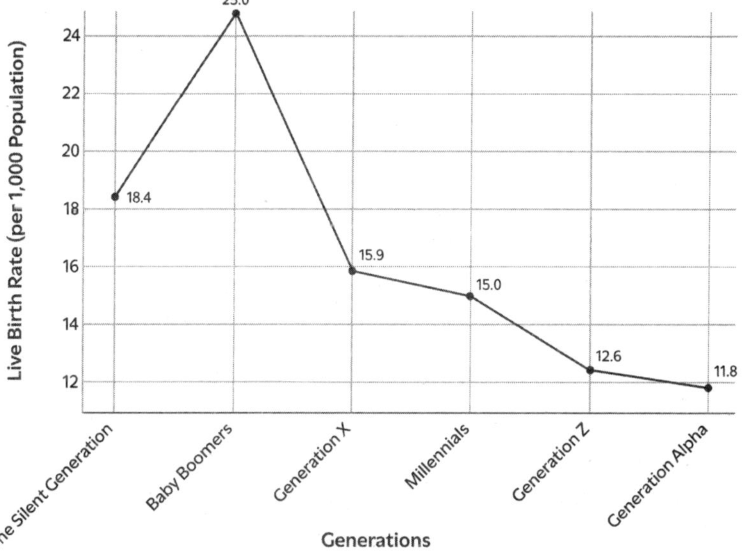

As women's access to education and career opportunities increased, many women began prioritizing their education and careers before starting a family. This delay in childbearing naturally led to lower birth rates. Greater access to contraception means women have more control over the timing and number of children they have.

Changes in lifestyle and personal preferences are another important factor. People marry later in life, which typically results in having children later and fewer children overall. Many individuals and couples prioritize personal goals, such as travel, career advancement, and personal development, over starting a family. This shift in priorities partially explains a growing trend toward smaller families, with many preferring to have one or two children rather than larger families, which were more common in previous generations.

Health and reproductive issues also play a role. Delayed childbearing correlates with increasing rates of infertility and can lead to challenges in conceiving, which reduces the overall birth rate. Rising awareness of health issues and the desire to provide a stable environment for children may also lead people to delay or reconsider having children.

Technological and environmental factors are further influencing the decline. Urban living, which often comes with higher costs and less space, can deter people from having larger families. Additionally, growing awareness of environmental issues and concerns about overpopulation and climate change may lead some individuals to choose to have fewer children.

The decline in the US birth rate reflects broader changes in society's values, economic conditions, and lifestyle choices. From a statistical point of view, we can't prove causation for any of these factors. But we do know that having children, or at least several children, does not reflect the priority of many Americans today. As we will see in more detail shortly, the decline of religion in general and church-based Christianity in particular has reflected the new values of culture almost simultaneously with the decline in the birth rate. Many parents of Gen Zers didn't take or send their children to church, because they viewed church as a family-centric institution that often focused on larger families. Indeed, many church ministries were centered on children and youth. It seemed that church was for larger and more traditional families.

Will Gen Alpha Be Similar to Gen Z, or Not?

As the two youngest generations, Gen Z and Gen Alpha are often compared for their distinctive traits and the environment in which they are growing up. Though both generations are heavily influenced by technology, their characteristics and experiences set them apart in several significant ways.

Both generations are digital natives, but their technology adoption differs significantly. Gen Z grew up during the rise of social media, smartphones, and the internet. Older members of Gen Z can remember a time before smartphones took over the world—but barely. And they adapted quickly to these technological advancements.

Gen Alpha, on the other hand, has been immersed in technology from birth, experiencing AI, smart devices, and the Internet of Things[12] from an early age. This constant exposure will make them even more tech-savvy than Gen Z and potentially even more alienated from in-person relationships.

The educational experiences of these generations also differ. Gen Z initially experienced a more traditional educational setting but saw a significant shift to online learning and digital tools, particularly during the COVID-19 pandemic. Gen Alpha has been integrated with digital learning tools, online resources, and educational apps from the start. Their education is more likely to include hybrid or fully digital classrooms—and not necessarily to their benefit.

When it comes to social media and communication, Gen Z predominantly uses platforms such as Instagram, Snapchat, and TikTok. They are adept at creating content and communicating through visual and short-form media. Though Gen Alpha is still young, they will likely use emerging platforms and newer forms of digital interaction, such as virtual reality and augmented reality.

The influence of parents also differentiates these two generations. Gen Z was raised by Gen X and older Millennials, with an upbringing focused on resilience, self-reliance, and dealing with economic uncertainty. In contrast, Gen Alpha is predominantly being raised by Millennials, who emphasize emotional intelligence, diversity, and inclusion. Millennial parents are highly engaged in their children's education and extracurricular activities, often leveraging technology to enhance those experiences.

Consumer behavior also shows differences between the two generations. Gen Z values *experiences* over material possessions and prefers brands that are ethical, sustainable, and socially responsible. Gen Alpha is projected to have similar values but will be even more discerning. Growing up with AI-driven personalization, they will expect highly customized shopping experiences and could be even more critical of brands' ethical and environmental records.

Though both generations are defined by their relationship with technology and global interconnectedness, Gen Alpha has been more deeply immersed in a digital world from birth. Their upbringing will emphasize emotional intelligence, global awareness, and personalized experiences, differentiating them from their Gen Z predecessors. As these young generations continue to evolve, understanding their unique characteristics will be crucial for shaping future societal trends and innovations.

We cannot assume that the two youngest generations will be similar in all respects. But all indications are that Gen Alpha will become an extension of the Anxious Generation.

2

FOUR THREATS TO OUR YOUNG PEOPLE

I LOVE MY GRANDCHILDREN. But I also worry about my grandchildren. Compared to many kids in our country today, my grandchildren are growing up with numerous advantages. They all have both parents in the home. Their parents love each other and are committed to each other and their families, and they model that love for their children.

All of my grandkids have both sets of grandparents still living—and doting on them. I am grateful for the parents of my three daughters-in-law. I'm not sure my grandchildren realize how blessed they are to have such love, encouragement, and support.

All of my grandkids are active in church, primarily because their parents are leading them that way. I will soon expand upon that theme, the main focus of this book, because the evidence is powerful. A young person active in church has a much better chance of coping with the unique challenges of their generation. We will unpack that reality in the chapters that follow.

Undoubtedly, the Rainer grandchildren have many advantages over some other young people. But they still struggle. They face the same temptations and pressures as their peers and from their peers. They are in the same cultural mess as everyone else. That is, my grandchildren are not immune to the problems I will note in this chapter. And that is a cause for concern.

I refer to these harms as "the big four," though my list is neither exhaustive nor conclusive. Still, the evidence is strong about the adverse effects of these four cultural threats. Sadly, I see their negative influence on my grandchildren and the rest of their generations.

The big four are *high-speed internet*, *smartphones*, *social media*, and *polarization*. The first three are building blocks that lay the foundation for the fourth. For better or worse, the internet provides immediate and unlimited access to information. It is truly the information superhighway. The smartphone is one of the vehicles that travels the information superhighway, offering constant, portable access to the growing and sometimes detrimental influence of the internet. Social media existed before the smartphone, but social media access became instant and ubiquitous with the advent of the smartphone.

Am I using a bit of hyperbole when I say that the big four are destroying our young people? Perhaps. Yet, the evidence seems overwhelming that the harm is great—certainly too great to ignore.

Please don't overlook the underlying research that shows the impact the big four have on young people.

Threat #1: The Internet

The internet, a revolutionary development in human history, transformed how we live, work, and communicate. Its origins trace back to the late 1960s with the creation of ARPANET, a project funded by the US Department of Defense.[1]

The purpose was to develop a decentralized network to maintain communications during a nuclear attack. The internet evolved through the 1980s and 1990s with the introduction of a domain name system (DNS), electronic mail, and eventually the development of the World Wide Web by Tim Berners-Lee. This innovation made the internet accessible to the general public, allowing information to be shared globally with unprecedented ease.

By the mid-1990s, the internet had become a household name, rapidly integrating into everyday life. The development of search engines such as Google and social media platforms such as Facebook, Twitter (now X), and Instagram further revolutionized how we interact with the world and each other. For those born after 1996—Gen Z and Gen Alpha—the internet has been ubiquitous, profoundly shaping their formative years.

Though online connectivity has undoubtedly brought numerous benefits, such as instant access to information, improved communication, and new educational tools, it also harbors significant risks, especially for young people. These risks can be broadly categorized into several areas.

Cyberbullying and Harassment

The anonymity and reach of the internet have, unfortunately, made it a breeding ground for cyberbullying and harassment. Many young people have experienced some form of online bullying.

The impact of such experiences can be severe, leading to anxiety, depression, and in extreme cases, suicidal thoughts. The persistence and public nature of online harassment can make it particularly damaging, as it follows the victim into what should be safe spaces, such as their homes.

Inappropriate Content

The vast expanse of the internet means that young people can easily stumble upon or be deliberately exposed to inappropriate content, including violence, pornography, and extremist ideologies. This exposure can distort their understanding of healthy relationships, personal safety, and social norms. The ease of access to such content has increased concerns about its impact on young minds, shaping their perceptions and behaviors in potentially harmful ways.

Addiction and Mental Health Issues

Internet addiction is a growing concern, with many young people spending excessive amounts of time online. This can lead to sleep deprivation, poor academic performance, and a lack of physical activity.

Moreover, the constant comparison with idealized images on social media can result in low self-esteem and body image issues. The need for validation through likes and shares can create a cycle of dependency, affecting overall mental well-being.

Privacy and Security Risks

Young people often share personal information online without fully understanding the privacy and security implications. This sharing can lead to identity theft, stalking, and other forms of exploitation. The permanence of online posts means that youthful indiscretions can have long-lasting consequences. In an age where personal data is valuable, understanding and protecting one's digital footprint has become crucial.

Disinformation and Radicalization

The internet is rife with disinformation, which can mislead young people and shape their views based on falsehoods. Additionally, extremist groups have been known to use the internet to radicalize vulnerable individuals, leading to dangerous behaviors and ideologies. The spread of fake news and conspiracy theories can create distorted worldviews, influencing everything from health decisions to political beliefs.

For those who are not digital natives, it is difficult to comprehend the pervasive influence of the internet on younger people who were not alive in the pre-internet era. When I look at my grandchildren, I see our biological similarities, our similar mannerisms, and our shared love for family. But I know that my grandchildren are different from my wife and me. They are different from our children. Our grandchildren were born and raised in a different culture, the internet culture. There are many benefits to being a digital native. However, there are far too many challenges for these young people.

Threat #2: Smartphones

Smartphones have become an inseparable part of daily life for most young people. The younger generations have grown up with instant access to information, communication, and entertainment all at their fingertips.

However, the perils accompanying this technology are profound and multifaceted. I noted earlier Jonathan Haidt's insightful book *The Anxious Generation*, where he delves deeply into the psychological and social challenges posed by the smartphone era, highlighting the urgency of addressing these issues.[2] While I noted some of the challenges related to the internet in general, the widespread use of smartphones takes the concerns to a new level.

Psychological Impact and Mental Health

Haidt emphasizes a startling correlation between the rise of smartphones and the increase in mental health issues among teenagers. Apple introduced the smartphone in 2007, and the iPhone 4 (2010) was the first model to feature a front-facing camera, making selfies a new thing just as the eldest members of Gen Z were entering adolescence. By 2013, a majority of US households had adopted the smartphone, coinciding with the rapid deterioration of mental health among young people—marked by alarming increases in rates of depression, anxiety, and self-harm.

Haidt argues that constant connectivity and social comparison (especially among girls) exacerbated these issues. Teenagers are bombarded with images and posts portraying idealized lives, leading to feelings of inadequacy and isolation.

Social media access through smartphones plays a significant role in this phenomenon. Platforms such as Instagram, Snapchat, and TikTok create environments where the number of likes, comments, and followers becomes a measure of self-worth. This relentless pursuit of validation can erode self-esteem and foster anxiety. Haidt points out that the pressure to present a perfect online persona often leads to stress and mental exhaustion.

After almost no change in the historical percentage of depression in teens prior to 2010, the numbers began to soar around 2012. As the chart at the top of the next page shows, major depression among boys increased by 161 percent within ten years, and by 145 percent among girls.[3]

The second graph is breathtaking. Look at the jump in anxiety prevalence by age group. In simple terms, the younger you are, the greater the likelihood you will have anxiety. Sadly, younger age groups in the future will likely carry this same level of anxiety.[4]

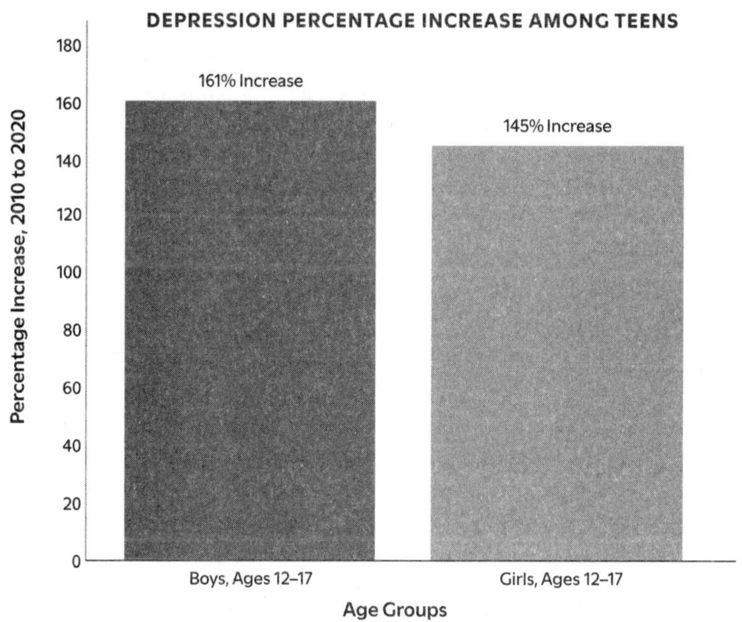
DEPRESSION PERCENTAGE INCREASE AMONG TEENS
Percentage Increase, 2010 to 2020
180
160
140
120
100
80
60
40
20
0
161% Increase
145% Increase
Boys, Ages 12–17
Girls, Ages 12–17
Age Groups

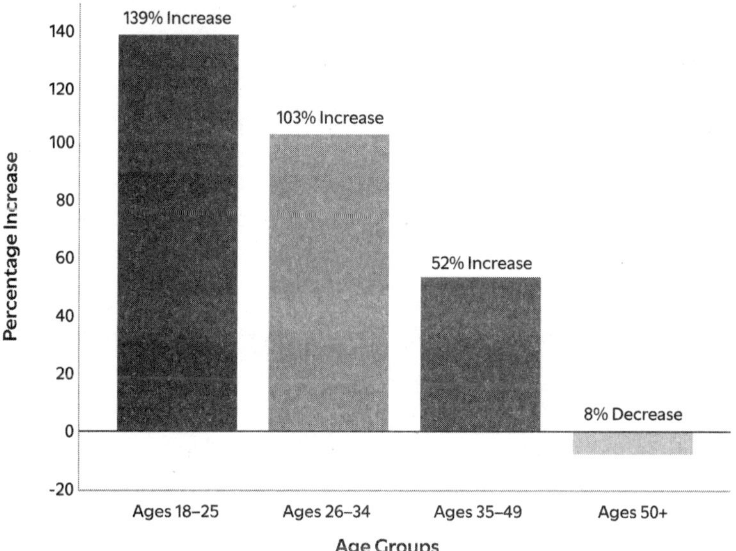
ANXIETY INCREASES BY AGE FROM 2010 TO 2020
Percentage Increase
140
120
100
80
60
40
20
0
-20
139% Increase
103% Increase
52% Increase
8% Decrease
Ages 18–25
Ages 26–34
Ages 35–49
Ages 50+
Age Groups

Because anxiety and depression are self-reported in surveys, there was some initial doubt about the veracity of claims that these maladies were increasing. Isn't it possible, the skeptics argued, that the increase in these numbers reflects young people becoming more open and willing to talk about these issues?

Two sad but cogent realities have powerfully countered that skepticism, backed by data from non-self-reported incidents. The number of emergency room visits by girls and boys for self-harm increased dramatically from 2010 to 2020. Likewise, suicide rates for girls and boys rose sharply during the same period.

The chart below paints a sad picture. The number of boys who ended up in emergency rooms because they attempted self-harm increased 48 percent from 2010 to 2020, while the number of girls who attempted self-harm rose 188 percent in the same period.[5]

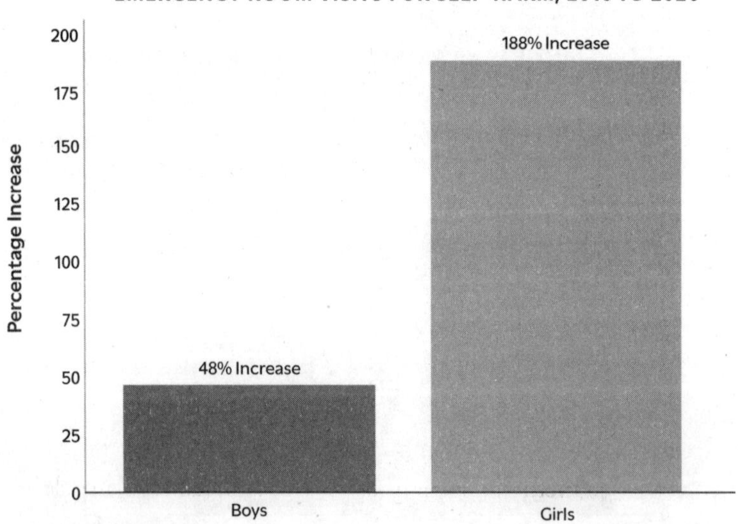

These reports of self-harm include adolescents treated for nonfatal injuries. But a report of suicide rates among boys and girls ages

10 to 14 reminds us that some of the injuries are fatal. Among the boys, the suicide rate increased by 91 percent from 2010 to 2020. Among the girls, the increase in the same period was an alarming 167 percent. In other words, suicide rates among girls nearly tripled.[6]

SUICIDE RATES FOR YOUNGER ADOLESCENTS

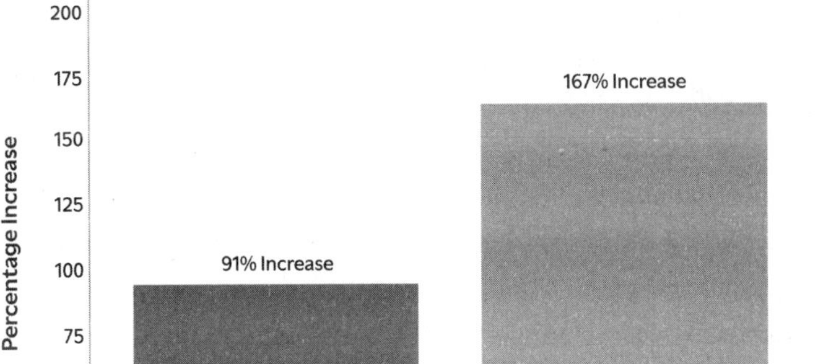

Correlation doesn't prove causation, of course. But researchers will often assume causation if a number of evidentiary factors are present. Without getting into the tedious details, there is clear evidence that smartphone use harms our kids in several critical ways.

Sleep Deprivation and Cognitive Effects

Sleep deprivation is another critical challenge posed by smartphone use. The blue light emitted by smartphone screens interferes with the production of melatonin, a hormone that regulates sleep. This disruption can lead to difficulties falling asleep and staying asleep, particularly among teenagers predisposed to irregular sleep patterns due to biological changes.

Haidt notes that sleep deprivation has a cascade of adverse effects on cognitive function, emotional regulation, and overall well-being. Lack of adequate sleep can impair memory, attention, and decision-making skills, making it harder for students to perform academically. Additionally, chronic sleep deprivation is linked to mood disorders, further exacerbating the mental health crisis among young people.[7]

Cyberbullying and Online Harassment

The smartphone, while a tool for connection, also opens the door to cyberbullying and online harassment. Unlike traditional bullying, which is confined to specific locations and times, cyberbullying can occur anytime and anywhere, thanks to the smartphone. Victims of cyberbullying often feel they have no safe space, as the harassment invades their homes and personal time.

Haidt's research underscores the severe psychological impact of cyberbullying. Victims are at a higher risk of experiencing depression, anxiety, and even suicidal ideation. The anonymity provided by online platforms emboldens bullies, who may not fully grasp the consequences of their actions on their victims. The pervasive nature of cyberbullying necessitates robust interventions and support systems for affected individuals.

Addiction and Reduced Physical Activity

Smartphones are *designed* to be addictive. Features such as notifications, endless scrolling, and instant gratification create a compulsion to check the device frequently. This compulsion can lead to significant reductions in physical activity, as young people spend more time glued to their screens and less time engaging in outdoor play and exercise.

Young people often ignore people around them in favor of their smartphones. This behavior can strain interpersonal relationships and diminish face-to-face social skills. The reduction in physical activity also has broader health implications, contributing to the rise in obesity and related health issues among teenagers. These same concerns affect smartphone users of all ages, but adolescents and children are still in their formative years, which supercharges the negative effects on their development.

Privacy Concerns and Digital Footprint

The ease of sharing information via smartphones raises significant privacy concerns. Young people often share personal details online without fully understanding the long-term implications. Photos, videos, and posts can become part of a permanent digital footprint, potentially affecting future educational and employment opportunities.

Though smartphones offer unparalleled convenience and connectivity, they also pose significant challenges and dangers for Gen Z and Gen Alpha. The psychological impact, exacerbation of mental health issues, sleep deprivation, cyberbullying, addiction, and privacy concerns are critical areas that require attention. Jonathan Haidt provides a compelling examination of these issues, urging parents, educators, and policymakers to take proactive steps in mitigating the risks associated with smartphone use. For that reason, I strongly encourage you to read *The Anxious Generation*. It will open your eyes to this "great rewiring of childhood" (Haidt's phrase). And it will give you a dose of healthy fear.

Threat #3: Social Media

Three of my grandsons are with me today as I write this chapter. The eldest one loves to converse with me about five topics: sports, religion, politics, family history, and YouTube.

Frankly, when my grandchildren were born, I never expected I would ever have prolonged conversations with any of them about YouTube. This particular grandchild has his own YouTube channel. He has focused the channel well to attract a specific audience. He is excited about his number of subscribers, views, and likes.

Yes, it's a different world.

Though I love my time with my grandson on any topic, his infatuation with this one avenue of social media indicates how social media can draw anyone in, especially adolescents in their formative years.

Kids today are growing up in a digital age where social media feels integral to their daily lives. While social media platforms offer opportunities for connection, learning, and entertainment, several negative issues should not be overlooked, especially for adolescents.

These issues can adversely affect their mental health, development, and overall well-being. Some will exacerbate the problems I noted with the internet and smartphones.

Mental Health Concerns

One of the more significant adverse effects of social media use on adolescents is related to mental health. Multiple studies have shown that heavy social media use is associated with increased rates of depression, anxiety, and stress among teenagers. The consequences affect boys and girls differently, but both groups are significantly impacted.

A study published in *JAMA Psychiatry* found that adolescents who spend more than three hours per day on social media are at a higher risk for mental health problems, including internalizing problems like anxiety and depression. The constant comparison with peers, exposure to idealized images, and cyberbullying are only some of the factors contributing to these mental health issues.[8]

Cyberbullying

Cyberbullying is a prevalent problem on social media platforms. Unlike traditional bullying, cyberbullying can occur 24/7, with no escape for the victim. Adolescents who experience cyberbullying often report higher levels of emotional distress, depression, and anxiety.

According to a report by the Cyberbullying Research Center, approximately 55 percent of students have experienced cyberbullying at some point.[9] The anonymity provided by social media can embolden bullies and exacerbate the impact on victims.

Body Image Issues

Social media often presents an unrealistic portrayal of beauty and body standards. Adolescents who are already vulnerable to body image issues may develop negative self-perceptions and unhealthy behaviors in an attempt to emulate these ideals.

A major study of eating disorders found that social media use is linked to body dissatisfaction and disordered eating behaviors among teens. The prevalence of edited and filtered images can create a distorted sense of reality, making adolescents feel inadequate and dissatisfied with their appearance.[10]

Sleep Disturbance

Excessive use of social media, especially before bedtime, can interfere with sleep patterns. In addition to the blue light sleep disruption problem I noted earlier, the engagement and excitement generated by social media interactions can make it difficult for adolescents to unwind and fall asleep. A major study on sleep disorders revealed that adolescents who use social media heavily are more likely to suffer from sleep disturbances, affecting their academic performance and overall health.[11]

Addiction and Reduced Attention Span

The addictive algorithms behind social media platforms intentionally make it difficult for people to stop scrolling. Even when users log off, notifications remind them of what they're missing. Adolescents may develop an unhealthy dependency on social media, leading to reduced attention spans and difficulty concentrating on tasks.

The constant need to check updates and notifications can interfere with academic responsibilities and face-to-face interactions. Multiple studies indicate that social media addiction is becoming increasingly common among teenagers, adversely affecting their academic performance and social skill development.

Privacy and Security Risks

Adolescents often share personal information on social media without fully understanding the privacy implications. This can expose them to risks such as identity theft, online predators, and unwanted attention.

The lack of awareness about privacy settings and the potential for oversharing can make adolescents vulnerable to exploitation and cyber threats. A study by the Pew Research Center found that many teens are concerned about the privacy of their information on social media, yet many still engage in risky online behaviors.[12]

Isolation

Though social media can facilitate communication, it can also hinder the development of face-to-face social skills. Adolescents may become overly reliant on digital interactions, leading to a decrease in meaningful in-person relationships. This can affect their ability to develop empathy, communication skills, and emotional intelligence. Excessive social media use can lead to social isolation and difficulties in forming and maintaining offline relationships.

Threat #4: Polarization

The polarization of society, characterized by increasing divisions along political, social, and cultural lines, significantly affects adolescents. This polarization, exacerbated by social media, partisan news outlets, and political rhetoric, influences young people in several ways, including their mental health, social interactions, and perspectives on the world.

Emotional Well-being

Polarization contributes to heightened stress and anxiety among adolescents. The constant exposure to divisive and often hostile political discourse can create a sense of instability and fear.

Adolescents are particularly vulnerable because they are in a developmental stage where they are forming their identities and values. Political polarization can exacerbate feelings of stress and anxiety in young people, particularly those who are deeply engaged in political issues.

Moreover, the us-versus-them mentality fostered by polarization can lead to internal conflicts, especially for adolescents who belong to families or communities with differing viewpoints. This environment can create pressure to conform to specific beliefs, leading to anxiety and a fear of social ostracism.

Social Relationships and Interpersonal Skills

Polarization also affects adolescents' social relationships and interpersonal skills. The divisive nature of contemporary society often spills over into personal interactions, making it challenging for young people to engage in open and respectful dialogue. Teens often report experiencing conflicts with friends and family members over political issues, which can strain relationships.

Influence of Social Media on Polarization

Social media plays a crucial role in amplifying societal polarization and its impact on adolescents. Algorithms designed to maximize engagement often promote sensational, divisive, or extreme content. Adolescents who are heavy users of social media are thus regularly exposed to polarized content that can shape their views and attitudes. Adolescents who frequently use social media are more likely to encounter and be influenced by politically polarized content.

Identity Formation and Civic Engagement

The polarization of society also affects the process of identity formation among adolescents. As young people navigate their developing sense of self, they are influenced by the polarized messages they receive from media, peers, and family. This influence can lead to a fragmented identity where political beliefs overshadow other aspects of their personality.

Educational Environment

The impact of societal polarization is also felt within educational settings. Teachers and administrators often struggle to address controversial issues without appearing biased, which can lead to a lack of comprehensive civic education. This gap in education can leave adolescents ill-equipped to analyze political information and engage in informed discussions critically.

Moreover, the polarization of society can create a hostile environment in schools, where students feel unsafe expressing their views. This atmosphere can stifle free speech and discourage students from exploring different perspectives critical for their intellectual and social development.

I have devoted a significant portion of this book to describing the challenges facing all of us, but especially Gen Z and Gen Alpha. Yes, the situation is difficult, often dire. And though I know that many of the resources available to help these young people are invaluable, one resource has been largely silent in this discussion—namely, the local church. That conspicuous silence may be the greatest travesty for these young people.

So let's turn our attention to the local church as a key resource and help for Gen Z and Gen Alpha. Yes, the local church brings its own problems and challenges to the situation. Since Jesus ascended into heaven, the local church has been his plan for reaching the world with the Good News of the gospel. But no local church has ever done it perfectly.

Nevertheless, despite its weaknesses in many cases, I believe the local church offers the greatest help and resource for struggling young people.

Let's see what might happen when the Anxious Generation goes to church.

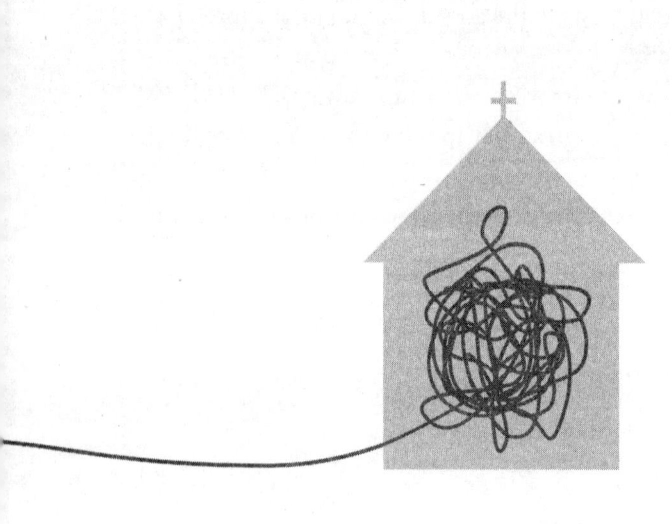

3

SHOULD THE ANXIOUS GENERATION GO TO CHURCH?

I BEGAN MY CAREER AS A BUSINESSMAN, and I was successful. While still in our twenties, my wife and I had the comforts of material wealth and prestige beyond anything we'd ever imagined. From the outside, our life was one of success and attainment.

But God began to move us in another direction. I wish I could adequately explain how he did that. There were some circumstances that nudged us to leave the business world for vocational ministry, but the primary reason I left was an internal certainty that we must respond positively to God even if the direction didn't quite make sense to us.

To my knowledge, my family tree includes no other pastors or vocational ministers. So why me? Nellie Jo and I yielded to a certainty that we were to step out in faith, even though we had no idea where it would lead. To be clear, it was an unlikely path. We sold almost everything we owned and moved to a seminary where we spent the next six years preparing for ministry. I was ready to end my formal studies after earning a master's degree, but Nellie Jo encouraged me to stay and complete a PhD as well.

My ministry training included the usual fare of New Testament, Old Testament, Greek, Hebrew, church history, theology, and the like. But I found myself particularly drawn to the role of the local church and centered as much of my studies as possible there. All my elective courses had that focus. I researched and wrote as many papers as I could on the local church, and my PhD dissertation focused on the evangelistic expansion of the early church and the contemporary church.

After seminary, I served as a pastor of four churches. When I later became dean of a seminary, I shaped degrees with an emphasis on the local church. So I feel as if I know a thing or two about the local church.

Is the Church the Answer for the Anxious Generation?

Is the church *really* the answer for the Anxious Generation? It's a fair and honest question to ask. Given how the local church pervades my life story and has long been my passion, you would probably expect me to answer in the affirmative. But I also want to be objective, at least as objective as my background will allow. I want to share with you my transparent and unvarnished view of the local church in America—though I have also kept up with churches worldwide.

I will begin with a blunt admission: The church is not a silver bullet for the Anxious Generation. You will not find a church without flaws. Sometimes the flaws are significant. Sometimes the actions of Christians in churches are cringeworthy.

Therefore, I must begin any argument in favor of the local church by admitting those flaws. Though most churches are relatively healthy in many parts of the world, the majority of churches in the United States are struggling. It's worth our time to look at their plight to understand the challenges we must overcome.

Churches in Decline

It may seem ironic that I would point the struggling Anxious Generation to churches that are struggling themselves. Indeed, churches in America have been in decline for several decades by now. In the approximately 375,000 churches in the United States, attendance has steadily declined over the past twenty-five years. Whereas median worship attendance was 137 in 2000, by 2025 it had declined to fifty. In other words, half the churches in America today have fewer than fifty people in attendance. That's a drop of 63 percent since 2000![1]

MEDIAN WORSHIP ATTENDANCE OF CHURCHES IN THE US

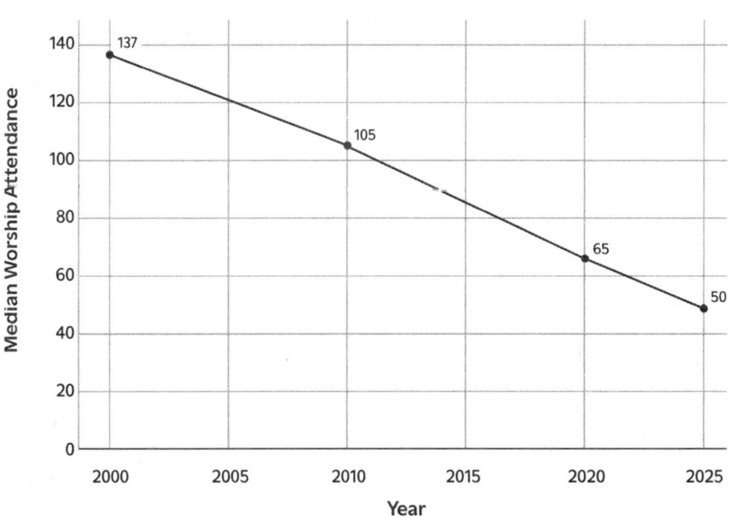

Some of the decline occurred due to migration from smaller churches to larger churches. But unfortunately, most of the decline reflects the reality that fewer people today are going to church.

Numerical measurements may not be the best way to determine the health of the church; but in my forty years of research on the local church, I have not found a better indicator for broad application.

During my teenage years, when I was not a regular church attender, I used a common excuse that is still prevalent today: The church is the *people*, not the building. The inference, of course, is that you don't have to attend a worship service to be a faithful member of a church.

The problem with that statement is that it's not fully biblical. Of course the church comprises the people of God, whether they are in a building or not. But the Bible is clear that God's people have always *gathered somewhere* regularly to worship together. The first church in Jerusalem "worshiped together at the Temple each day."[2] They worshiped *together*, and they worshiped at a specific place.

So, let's be honest. If the Anxious Generation goes to church in America, they will likely go to a church that is in decline. But this might be the shot in the arm those churches need to regain their footing and their sense of hope and purpose. What the Anxious Generation needs as much as anything is a personal connection with people who care. They need to hear the gospel truth that God loves them, Jesus is their Rock and their Redeemer, and the Holy Spirit is their guide. And every Bible-believing church has that to offer. As Jesus told Peter, "I will build my church, and all the powers of hell will not conquer it."[3] That is a powerful promise from our Lord and Savior.

Pathways to Growth

A church can grow its attendance in four ways: *biologically*, *demographically*, through *transfers*, and through *conversions*.[4]

Biological growth occurs when church members grow their families and bring their children to church. Family oriented, intergenerational churches tend to grow biologically.

Demographic growth occurs when new residents move into a community and start going to church. Demographic growth is the most common among faster-growing churches.[5] As communities grow, so do some of the churches in those communities.

Transfer growth refers to church members moving from one church to another in the same community. Tongue in cheek, we call it "the circulation of the saints." In many communities, it's not uncommon to find a popular—and typically larger—church attracting members from other churches with high-level worship services, programs, and facilities. These churches typically remain popular for about a decade before the attraction wears off.

Conversion growth takes place when churches reach non-Christians. It is the type of growth foreseen by the Great Commission and the type of growth Jesus commanded. Right before Jesus left earth, he said, "You will receive power when the Holy Spirit comes upon you. And you will be my witnesses, telling people about me everywhere—in Jerusalem, throughout Judea, in Samaria, and to the ends of the earth."[6] Conversion growth is biblical growth. An obedient church reaches people who are not Christians. An obedient church will reach the Anxious Generation, both Christians and non-Christians.

Biological growth can add to a church's attendance, but with the declining birth rate in our society, most churches in America today have a higher death rate than birth rate. The church is aging, so this trend will likely accelerate.

Demographic and transfer growth mean that some churches gain at the expense of others. Thus, there is no net gain for the Kingdom.

From a biblical perspective, only conversion growth results in a healthy, growing church. It is the only growth mentioned in the New Testament and the only growth that Christ commands.

We don't have any data to show how many conversions there are each year across all 375,000 churches in America. When we first started measuring conversion growth, we used conversions and membership as our guide. For example, if a church of two hundred in attendance had twenty conversions in a year, we would say that church had a 10:1 conversion rate. Or we would say it takes ten members a year to reach one person for Christ. The lower the ratio the better.

Because many church membership rolls became inflated and inaccurate over time, we started comparing attendance to conversions. A church with an average of one hundred in worship attendance and five conversions in a year would have a 20:1 conversion ratio. Again, the lower the ratio the better. The problem with this approach is that a church could have fewer conversions and yet have a better conversion ratio if attendance dropped significantly.

When we do church consultations, we try to determine how many *active* members the church has. We consider someone an active member if they attend worship at least once a month. So we calculate the conversion ratio based on active members. A church with an active membership of three hundred that has eight conversions a year has a conversion ratio of 37.5:1 (300 divided by 8).

Okay, enough with the numerical details. I just want you to know how we attempt to measure conversion growth since it is our way of assessing the biblical growth of a particular church.

Using the formula just mentioned, here are our estimates for average conversion growth in America since 1980.[7] Remember, the ratio reflects the number of church members it takes to achieve one conversion per year.

- 1980 41:1
- 1990 50:1
- 2000 62:1
- 2010 78:1
- 2019 86:1
- 2024 93:1

In 1980, it took forty-one church members to reach one convert in a year. If we're at all serious about the Great Commission, that number is not encouraging. But by 2024, the situation was much worse. It took ninety-three members to reach one convert in a year.

Church leaders and church members know they are not reaching people for Christ at a healthy rate. Whenever we at Church Answers do one of our Know Your Church perception studies (which we've been doing since 1996), asking church members to evaluate their church in six areas—worship, prayer, discipleship, fellowship, ministry, and evangelism—evangelism scores the lowest, with few exceptions.

Other Measures

There are possibly other ways to measure church health. For example, we have a tool that can measure the biblical knowledge of church members and leadership. But does that truly measure health?

I recently completed a church consultation where the pastor and other church leaders demonstrated vast biblical knowledge. Their scores on our survey affirmed our initial impressions. These leaders knew the Bible backward and forward. But the reason the church had called us was its steady decline in attendance, finances, and building maintenance. The leaders knew the Bible, but they largely ignored the biblical mandate to reach people who are not Christians. Knowledge did not result in obedience.

We could possibly attempt to gauge church health in such areas as unity, love, and discipleship. But we face the same challenges. How do we accurately measure these important matters on a widespread basis? And do they truly indicate church health?

We therefore concluded that the attendance metrics—and, to some degree, the conversion metrics—are sufficient for determining whether a church is on a healthy trajectory. And based on personal experience, I can say conclusively that, by and large, churches in America are declining in health. Even so, I am willing to open the doors of these unhealthy churches to the Anxious Generation. Indeed, I am eager to get these young people into our churches. And I assure you I am not living in fantasyland.

Getting to the Bottom Line

Let's conclude this chapter by answering the question in the title: *Should the Anxious Generation go to church?* Contrary to what might seem like common sense, I can answer that question without hesitation. *Yes*, the Anxious Generation should go to church.

My point in showing the decline and lack of health in churches was to let you know that I'm fully aware of the issues that many congregations face today. So let me briefly address why I encourage churches to reach out to these young people despite all the challenges.

First, no church is perfect, even a relatively healthy church. Church members are sinners—forgiven sinners, to be clear, but sinners nonetheless. But that reality should serve to keep us humble. We should never consider ourselves better than others. We are forgiven but not perfect. Because the church by definition is the sum of its members, the church is not perfect either.

Second, the steps that are necessary to reach the Anxious Generation are steps in the direction of church health. Given that Jesus commissioned the church to make disciples of all the nations, making room for the Anxious Generation is part of biblical obedience. The antidote to weak, toxic, or declining churches is churches that are growing, sowing seed, and going into the world to preach the gospel. Jesus hasn't given up on the local church, and neither should we. Let this be a wake-up call, if needed, to get your church in line with God's purpose in the world—a purpose that certainly includes reaching the Anxious Generation.

Third, the Bible tells us clearly that churches can be messed up—but God can use them anyway to advance his cause. Here are a few examples:

Disagreements vs. Faithful and Joyful Generosity

> Your faithful service is an offering to God. And I want all of you to share that joy. Yes, you should rejoice, and I will share your joy.
>
> PHILIPPIANS 2:17-18

> Whatever happens, my dear brothers and sisters, rejoice in the Lord.
>
> PHILIPPIANS 3:1

> Now I appeal to Euodia and Syntyche. Please, because you belong to the Lord, settle your disagreement.
>
> PHILIPPIANS 4:2

As you know, you Philippians were the only ones who gave me financial help when I first brought you the Good News and then traveled on from Macedonia. No other church did this.

PHILIPPIANS 4:15

Sexual Immorality and Divisiveness vs. Unity, Love, and the Gifts of the Spirit

I appeal to you, dear brothers and sisters, by the authority of our Lord Jesus Christ, to live in harmony with each other. Let there be no divisions in the church.

1 CORINTHIANS 1:10

It's not important who does the planting, or who does the watering. What's important is that God makes the seed grow. The one who plants and the one who waters work together with the same purpose. And both will be rewarded for their own hard work.

1 CORINTHIANS 3:7-8

I can hardly believe the report about the sexual immorality going on among you.

1 CORINTHIANS 5:1

There are different kinds of spiritual gifts, but the same Spirit is the source of them all. There are different kinds of service, but we serve the same Lord. God works in different ways, but it is the same God who does the work in all of us.

A spiritual gift is given to each of us so we can help each other.

1 CORINTHIANS 12:4-7

The human body has many parts, but the many parts make up one whole body. So it is with the body of Christ. Some of us are Jews, some are Gentiles, some are slaves, and some are free. But we have all been baptized into one body by one Spirit, and we all share the same Spirit.
1 CORINTHIANS 12:12-13

Three things will last forever—faith, hope, and love—and the greatest of these is love.
1 CORINTHIANS 13:13

Quarrels and Fights vs. Drawing Close to God and Praying in Faith

What is causing the quarrels and fights among you?
JAMES 4:1

Humble yourselves before God. Resist the devil, and he will flee from you. Come close to God, and God will come close to you. . . . Humble yourselves before the Lord, and he will lift you up in honor.
JAMES 4:7-8, 10

A prayer offered in faith will heal the sick, and the Lord will make you well. And if you have committed any sins, you will be forgiven.

Confess your sins to each other and pray for each other so that you may be healed. The earnest prayer of a righteous person has great power and produces wonderful results.
JAMES 5:15-16

Yes, the church has its problems and challenges. But amazingly God still uses the imperfect people of the church to advance his purpose in the world. The church offers the Anxious Generation a place where their lives can be changed for the better.

From Acts 2 to Revelation 3, the New Testament is either *about* the local church, written *to* the local church, or written in the *context* of the local church. I am excited to encourage the Anxious Generation to go to church because God uses our churches despite all our weaknesses. The Holy Spirit is at work in the church, even when the church's members don't reflect the character of Christ.

As we dig a bit deeper into the needs of the Anxious Generation, we will discover that the local church can meet so many of their needs and be a salve to many of their wounds. Though the church is far from perfect, we will soon discover why it can be good for these young people to get involved there. But if the local church is so good for these young people, why are most of the young people not in church? Let us turn our attention to that question now.

4

WHY THE ANXIOUS GENERATION DOESN'T GO TO CHURCH

UBER IS NOW ONE OF MY FAVORITE MISSION FIELDS. I use the rideshare app frequently. Most of my trips are twenty minutes or less, and I'm amazed at how often I'm able to have a gospel conversation in such a short amount of time.

Keep in mind that I'm a classic introvert. These short trips would typically be quiet moments for me to recharge. Instead, I have asked God to give me opportunities to talk to the drivers about Jesus.

One of my more recent conversations was with Jacob, who told me he was born in 2000, making him a member of Gen Z and the Anxious Generation. I usually start my conversations by asking the drivers if they are from the city where they picked me up. From there, I ask if they have a church home. From that point on, the conversation takes an amazingly consistent path.

In Jacob's case, his responses were predictable for a Gen Zer. He didn't have a church home, but without my asking, he told me he believed in God. He didn't think religion could be confined to a building or an institution. He prays almost every week. His parents went to church occasionally when he lived at home, but they never pushed him to go. He's not an atheist, because he can't see how the world was created or exists today without someone in charge.

At that point, I shared with him that Christianity is not a religion but a personal relationship with Jesus Christ. I told him the meaning of the Cross for the forgiveness of sins. I shared with him how the Resurrection gives us the promise of eternal life. And I let him know he could have a relationship with God by confessing that he is a sinner and accepting the free gift of salvation through Christ. When we reached my destination, I thanked him, wished him well, and got out of the car.

Of the many rideshares I've taken, only once has the driver not wanted to talk about his beliefs. And even he was polite about it.

I keep an eye on my rider ratings to see if any of my gospel conversations result in a low score. My current rating is 4.87 out of 5.00, so I don't think I've offended anyone too much.

The Attitudes of the Unchurched

Many years ago, I led a group in a major research project to assess the attitudes of the unchurched toward the church and Christians. That research is now dated, but I believe the results are still valid. We found that only 5 percent of the unchurched respondents had an antagonistic attitude toward Christians and the church.

For the most part, the unchurched among us don't hate

Christians. They don't hate God. They don't hate the church. If anything, they're indifferent.

My conversation with Jacob the Uber driver exemplified the Anxious Generation's perspective on God. He wasn't an atheist. He believed in the existence of God. He wasn't an agnostic—that is, someone who is uncertain about the existence of God. Jacob seemed to have little doubt that God existed, but he admitted he really didn't know much about him.

Jacob's attitude toward the church was, again, a classic Anxious Generation response. He believed it wasn't necessary to belong to an institution or go to a building to connect with God. In other words, we ought to be able to connect with God anywhere at any time. Thus the church is simply not necessary.

But perhaps worried that he might have offended me, Jacob made it clear he has nothing against Christians or those who attend church. "It's just not my thing," he said.

The Anxious Generation doesn't attend church because they haven't been given a compelling reason to go. Most of my rideshare drivers have told me that they rarely encounter Christians who want to talk about their faith. Jacob wondered why Christians are so reticent to discuss something that should be their highest priority.

My rideshare drivers almost always inform me that they pray. I'm not sure *who* they are praying to, if indeed they are atheists or agnostics; but, in any case, they pray.

The Nones and the Anxious Generation

Ryan Burge, a political science professor at Eastern Illinois University, studies the Nones more than any person I know. The Nones are people who don't identify with any specific religious tradition or denomination. Their religious affiliation or identification is "nothing in particular."

Burge has tracked the Nones for years. Here are the percentages of Nones of the total US population in selected years:

- 2008: 21 percent
- 2013: 30 percent
- 2018: 32 percent
- 2019: 35 percent
- 2020: 34 percent
- 2021: 36 percent
- 2022: 35 percent
- 2023: 36 percent[1]

The dramatic growth of the Nones from 21 percent of the United States population in 2008 to 30 percent in 2013 was newsworthy. The trend continued without much fanfare as the percentage increased to 35 percent. It looked like the Nones were on their way to taking over America.

Then the growth stopped. From 2019 to 2023, the Nones hit a ceiling between 34 percent and 36 percent. In 2023, Gen Z, representing the Anxious Generation, had a larger representation among the Nones, at 42 percent.[2]

The Nones seem to be the perfect description of the plurality of the Anxious Generation. They lean toward no religion in particular, and their attitude is one of indifference rather than negativity. It's not that they don't like Christians or churches; they just don't think about them all that much.

That said, the Anxious Generation *will* give you negative reasons why they don't go to church—if you give them choices. I mean, if you asked a good friend of mine to give you an open-ended opinion about me, I think he would include a lot of positive attributes. But if you gave him a list of negative things he could check off about me, I don't think the response sheet would come back empty. It's all in how you ask the questions.

Seeing that about half the Nones left the church before they turned eighteen, Ryan Burge led a study asking why they left or never connected with the church.[3] He offered a menu of options, and the respondents could select as many options as they desired. The results were mostly predictable.

WHY NONES LEFT OR NEVER CONNECTED WITH THE CHURCH

Religious hypocrisy	42 percent
Religion doesn't make sense	35 percent
Religious bigotry	31 percent
Harm caused by religion in the world	28 percent
Science	28 percent
Lack of evidence	25 percent
Prejudice against LGBTQ people	24 percent
Harm caused by religion to me or people I know	19 percent
I moved away and never went back	11 percent
Reading the Bible	9 percent
Reading skeptical authors	6 percent
Other reasons	5 percent

Though I believe these responses were truthful, our further research at Church Answers indicates there is more to Gen Z's leaving the church than a list of negative reasons.

Digging Deeper

Springtide Research Institute conducted a massive study of young people ages thirteen to twenty-five.[4] In their report, they asked questions to more than ten thousand respondents in this demographic, which they said was the most extensive available data set for these young people in the United States.

The study aligns with other research on this generation. They have a general distrust of institutions, including churches. Our Church Answers research tells us the same thing. But there is a caveat. Their distrust of churches goes away when they get involved in a church. It appears that distrust is connected to disconnection. They don't know a church and the people in it, so they distrust all churches.

Their attitude is similar to the deep distrust of the US Congress noted in multiple studies. Though young people distrust the institution of Congress, they are more positive about their individual member of Congress and their Senators. They know their local political representatives, so the trust level is higher.

The Springtide project noted at several points that young people as a whole feel isolated and lonely. The introduction of the ubiquitous smartphone into their lives exacerbated their loneliness to degrees we could not have anticipated. Digital relationships could not adequately replace their in-person relationships.

It's no surprise, then, that the Springtide study noted that the introduction of one or more mentors to a young person's life had significant benefits. In-person relationships were critical to mitigating loneliness. It makes sense. Real people are better for us than people on a screen.

Is there more, then, to the low numbers of the Anxious Generation attending churches? Some of our research indicates there is indeed more to the story.

Surprising Insights about the Unchurched

My son Sam and I led a team at Church Answers Research to compare attitudes about the church between the unchurched and the churched.[5]

Before we peel back the layers of this study, let's look at our eleven major findings after we asked the same questions of two groups: those who attend church regularly and those who do not attend church regularly.

> **Finding 1:** *Unchurched does not always mean no church.* Many unchurched people have at least a distant or relational connection to a local church. Additionally, almost two-thirds (63 percent) of those not active in church today claim they were regular church attenders as children. For most of the unchurched, their views of the church are not detached from their personal experiences with the church.
>
> **Finding 2:** *The unchurched believe that churches are generally good for their communities.* Almost six out of ten unchurched people agree or strongly agree. Neither group had a negative general perception of churches.
>
> **Finding 3:** *The unchurched struggle to connect personally with the churches in their communities.* Though the unchurched have generally favorable views of the church as being good for society, that doesn't translate into a meaningful connection with churches in their local community. They like the idea of the church as a moral beacon, with the potential to do good, yet they remain unconvinced that the church is something for *them*. Only 38 percent

of the unchurched agree or strongly agree that they have a positive perception of churches in their local communities.

Finding 4: *The unchurched believe churches are still relevant but not trustworthy.* A significant surprise emerged in the data: Nonattenders view the church as more relevant today than churchgoers do. But the issue of trust is a different story. Attenders generally trust their churches (81 percent) and pastors (76 percent), while trust levels among nonattenders are lower with churches (30 percent) and pastors (35 percent).

Finding 5: *The unchurched are open to friendships through church but are intimidated to visit because they don't feel welcome.* Over half the nonattender respondents believed the church would be a good place to make new friends, but they are intimidated to visit a church alone.

Finding 6: *Confusion keeps the unchurched away more than church rules do.* Church rules are not a deterrent for the unchurched. Our study revealed only four out of ten unchurched people believe churches have too many rules. It's not the rules themselves but the lack of clarity about the church. More than 60 percent of unchurched people agree or strongly agree that churches are confusing for outsiders. Surprisingly, the same percentage of church attenders hold the same view. Both the churched and the unchurched agree that the church is confusing to outsiders.

Finding 7: *Higher confusion and lower trust levels mean the unchurched have doubts about raising their families and discovering their talents in the context of the church.*

While attenders overwhelmingly believe the church is a good place to raise families (85 percent) and discover their talents (75 percent), the unchurched do not share the same perception. Only 44 percent of the unchurched agree or strongly agree the church is a good place to raise families. Additionally, only 29 percent of the unchurched agree or strongly agree that the church is a good place to discover and grow their talents.

Finding 8: *The primary reason the unchurched don't attend is indifference—not busyness or antagonism.* We asked the unchurched why they don't attend church regularly. As expected, a variety of answers surfaced. However, some clear themes also emerged. They are not upset with the church or too busy for the church. They are mainly indifferent to the church.

Finding 9: *The catalyst for the unchurched to attend church is a spiritual and personal connection.* What is the prompt? What causes someone to start attending church? The answer to indifference is intentionality. The unchurched start attending to grow spiritually and because someone invited them. It's the combination of spiritual and personal connections.

Finding 10: *Churched people care more about worship style, programming, and denominational preferences than do the unchurched.* The top reason churched people attend a particular church is because someone invited them. Indeed, both the churched and unchurched attend a specific church primarily because someone invited them.

Finding 11: *The unchurched have a slightly stronger preference for nondenominational churches when selecting a congregation.* Baptist, Catholic, and Methodist congregations top the list for the churched.[6]

This information is rich in its implications. Here are five of the most significant findings.

Distrust Is Often Tied to Distance

The less we know about an institution or organization, the more likely we are to distrust it. The majority of the Anxious Generation are not connected to a local church. Indeed, they are in a cycle of distrust. The more distant they become, the more they distrust the church. The more they distrust the church, the more distant they become.

The obvious question is why did they distance themselves from the church in the first place? We will address that question later in the chapter.

Distrust of Churches in General Has Not Led to an Overall Decline in Spirituality

The term *spirituality* has a broad meaning. It could mean that someone prays, believing their petitions and pleas are heard by some higher power somewhere. It could refer to a pluralistic view of religion that holds that all sincere beliefs in God are equal. In other words, it's not about the nature of the god in whom we believe; it's the fact that we believe in some form of higher power that matters.

Spirituality could take on the form of agnosticism. That is, we're not sure if there is a god, but we're not sure there isn't. We have to be open to the possibility that a god exists.

Spiritual people may have emotional ties to churches in general, or denominations in particular, even if they have never attended those churches. They likely have relatives who attended the churches in the past or still attend them today.

There is really not a strong anti-spiritual movement in our society as much as there is an anti-religion movement. Indeed, there remains an openness to spiritual matters among the Anxious Generation.

Churches Are Still Perceived to Be Relevant

This finding is significant. If young people believe churches are relevant, they should be open to connecting with them. In our study, unchurched people viewed churches as more relevant than did church attenders. That was one of the biggest surprises in our research project.

But there is a disconnect. Relevance doesn't result in trust. The unchurched are more likely not to trust a church because they are not connected to a church. Fewer than four out of ten unchurched people have a favorable view of churches in their own communities.

Perceived Reasons Are Usually Not Actual Reasons

Get into a discussion with someone about the growing unchurched population in America, and you will likely hear two key talking points. First, the argument goes, people are more antagonistic to Christians and churches. They don't come to church because they don't like the institution or the people who attend.

Second, people are just too busy today. Getting an unchurched person to attend church is almost impossible because they are so busy doing other things. They don't have time to add one more thing to their plate.

Both perspectives are wrong. As noted earlier, only 5 percent of the unchurched population is antagonistic toward the church. While there is no denying the busyness of anyone today, people choose to do the things they view as important. If they are busy with sports instead of church, they have voted with their actions that sports are more important. The attitude that keeps people away is rarely antagonism or busyness. Instead, it is indifference. And they are indifferent because they have not been invited to a church to see what it is really like.

If You Invite Them, They Will Come

If more than half of nonattenders believe the church would be a good place to make new friends, but they are intimidated to visit a church alone, Christians who attend church should be motivated to invite every unchurched person they know, particularly young people, to church.

It's no surprise that the unchurched don't want to visit a church by themselves. Church is an unknown entity to them. It might be intimidating to walk in the door. Few people are eager to show up at a place they know little about. Or they may have preconceived notions they have to overcome.

When we did our research for the book *The Unchurched Next Door* several years ago, we found that 82 percent of the unchurched were at least somewhat likely to attend church if invited.[7] We found in subsequent works that the likelihood increases if someone will attend church with them. Other research aligns with our findings.

Connecting the Dots

Here's what we know so far. We know that young people are struggling. We know that the widespread adoption of the smartphone has exacerbated problems such as anxiety and depression. We know that rates of self-harm and suicide increased dramatically with the adoption of the smartphone and the explosion of social media as a cultural force.

We also know that many young people are lonely. They have not found meaningful connections online. On the contrary, digital connections often amplify feelings of loneliness.

We know that the Anxious Generation is not anti-church, even though they have negative feelings about the institutional church. We know that those negative feelings often derive from a lack of knowledge about churches because they don't attend them.

We further know that if we invite young people to church, they will likely accept our invitation if we will accompany them to church. Finally, we know that local churches can be the source of meaningful relationships that positively address issues of loneliness, anxiety, and depression.

If you invite them, they will come. If they come, their lives can be enhanced in innumerable ways.

Invite Your One

Several years ago, our team at Church Answers created a ministry called Invite Your One, which was intentionally designed to get church members to invite at least one person to church on a specific day.[8] The results have been nothing short of amazing.

One of the key benefits of the ministry was the excitement created when church members discovered that unchurched people were generally receptive to an invitation and that many would actually attend. We have numerous reports from churches that attest to the positive behavioral changes among church members.

Another significant benefit was the excitement in the church when attendance increased dramatically on the Invite Your One Sunday. We have reports of churches increasing their attendance between 20 percent and 50 percent on that particular day.

Of course, an intangible benefit was the cultural change in the church that resulted from a successful Invite Your One initiative.

Many churches reported a shift from an inward focus to an outward focus. What was particularly encouraging for many churches was the number of young people outside the church who accompanied their churched friends to church.

Thus, we can say with confidence that the Anxious Generation will come to church if we invite them. So why don't Christians invite the unchurched with greater consistency? And are there any lasting benefits for the Anxious Generation when they decide to attend church?

Those are two of the questions we will answer in the remaining chapters.

5

WHEN THE ANXIOUS GENERATION GOES TO CHURCH

JIM WAS A BROKEN MAN. His fourteen-year-old son was struggling with severe depression, and Jim was at his wits' end. Though the son had not attempted suicide, he had told his parents more than once that they would be better off without him. Those words pierced Jim's heart.

Jim caught up with me during a thirty-minute break at a conference where I was speaking, so there wasn't time for an extended conversation. I primarily listened. Jim and his wife loved their son deeply. They had sought the best mental health resources and expertise they could find. They were doing everything they knew to do, but their son had not improved.

I knew I was both inexperienced and unqualified to discuss mental health issues, but the least I could do was listen. Jim had read a book I wrote several years ago with my middle son, Art. *Raising Dad* is essentially an autobiography of Art's childhood and my parenting of him.[1] Jim could sense the love my son and I have for each other through the book. He had come to the conference with the hope that he could catch me for a few minutes of conversation.

By now it was almost time for me to speak again at the conference, and Jim had tears streaming down his face. Knowing that I would have to leave in just a minute or so, Jim asked me, "What can I do?"

Frankly, it was a question I wished he hadn't asked. I didn't have an easy answer for him. Indeed, at the moment, I was unsure if I had *any* answer for him. But I couldn't leave him without some direction.

My first response was to pray for him. Neither of us cared that there was a crowd milling around us. The need was too great for self-consciousness.

After my prayer, I could tell that Jim was still waiting for a more direct answer. What could he do? Remembering that he had told me at the outset of the conversation that he and his family did not attend church, I responded softly, "Jim, you and your family need to start going to church."

He nodded and thanked me, but as I walked toward the stage to speak, I wondered whether I had responded appropriately. Was my solution too simplistic? Had I offered a silver bullet when I knew full well that there wasn't a quick-fix solution to the years of pain in the life of Jim's son?

Later that day, I would find myself at peace with my suggestion. Jim was already seeking professional help for his son, and frankly the local church is God's plan A for reaching and caring for people—so why wouldn't it be our plan as well?

I don't know your motivation for reading this book. Maybe you're the parent of someone in the Anxious Generation. Maybe you picked up the book out of a sense of desperation. You might not attend church. You might not even be a Christian. Can church attendance really help your child? My answer is an unequivocal *yes*. The local church is a place where you can find a caring community who will encourage you in your relationship with God. And church attendance is especially beneficial if parents attend church with their children.

For now, I want you to understand some practical benefits of church attendance for your Gen Z or Gen Alpha child. We'll get to the eternal issues later, but I want you to understand clearly how church attendance can help you and your child today.

A Sense of Belonging

A sense of belonging is a fundamental human need, akin to our need for food and shelter. For Gen Z, whose lives are deeply intertwined with digital connections, this need can sometimes go unfulfilled in the physical world. Attending church provides a unique opportunity for young people to experience genuine community and connection.

When a Gen Zer steps into a church building, they are stepping into a community that often transcends typical social boundaries. They'll typically meet people of various ages, backgrounds, and experiences. This diversity can be enriching, providing perspective and wisdom they might not encounter elsewhere. More importantly, it gives them a place to feel accepted and valued for who they are.

Churches offer a sanctuary from the often judgmental and superficial nature of online interactions. In many churches, young people are encouraged to be themselves and share their struggles and triumphs without fear of ridicule or rejection. This acceptance fosters a deep sense of belonging, a feeling that they are an integral part of something greater than themselves.

Belonging to a church community also provides consistent support during life's inevitable ups and downs. A supportive network can make all the difference when facing personal challenges or crises. This network of faith-filled individuals provides not only emotional support but also practical help, be it through prayer, mentorship, or acts of service.

In essence, attending church can fill the void that digital connections often leave behind. It offers Gen Z a tangible, loving community where they can grow spiritually, emotionally, and socially. For parents wondering how to support their Gen Zer, encouraging regular church attendance can be a powerful step toward fostering a healthy sense of belonging.

Reduced Screen Time

Sadly, in today's digital age, screen time is an ever-present part of life, particularly for the Anxious Generation. From smartphones to tablets and laptops to smart TVs, screens dominate our daily routines. This constant exposure can lead to various issues, including reduced attention spans, disrupted sleep patterns, and even mental health challenges such as anxiety and depression. Encouraging church attendance can provide a much-needed break from this digital saturation.

When young people attend church, they engage in face-to-face interactions that foster authentic, meaningful connections. These in-person interactions are invaluable, providing an alternative to the often impersonal and fleeting nature of online communication. Gen Z members are immersed in an environment that prioritizes personal engagement over digital distraction during church services, youth groups, and other church-related activities.

Reduced screen time at church not only benefits their social skills but also their mental and emotional well-being. It offers a sanctuary where young people can be present in the moment, free from the constant notifications and pressures of social media. These changes can lead to improved focus, better sleep, and a more balanced lifestyle.

Church activities often include opportunities for physical movement and community service, reducing the time spent in front of screens. Whether participating in a youth group outing, engaging in volunteer work, or simply spending time in fellowship, these activities encourage a healthier, more active lifestyle.

Positive Role Models

In a world where celebrities and social media influencers often set the standards for behavior and success, finding genuinely positive role models for Gen Z can be challenging. However, church attendance offers a unique environment in which young people can encounter and be influenced by individuals who exemplify strong moral and ethical values.

Within the church community, Gen Zers can interact with a diverse group of people who live out their faith in tangible ways. From pastors and youth leaders to dedicated volunteers and church elders, these individuals provide living examples of integrity, compassion, and resilience. They demonstrate what it means to lead a life guided by faith, offering a counterbalance to the often superficial and materialistic role models found in popular culture.

These positive role models can profoundly affect young people's development. They provide guidance, mentorship, and encouragement, helping Gen Zers navigate the complexities of life with wisdom and grace. Through regular interactions and relationships built within the church, young people can see firsthand how to handle challenges, make ethical decisions, and contribute positively to their community.

Church attendance can be a valuable resource for parents seeking to provide their children with strong, positive influences. It connects Gen Z with individuals who not only talk about living a godly life but also actively demonstrate it through their actions and commitments. This exposure to positive role models can inspire and shape young minds in profoundly beneficial ways.

Prayer and Emotional Support

Having a support system can make all the difference in times of distress, uncertainty, or emotional turmoil. For the Anxious Generation, attending church can provide a powerful source of prayer and emotional support, often lacking in other areas of their lives. The church community offers a safe space where young people can express their fears, hopes, and struggles, knowing they will be met with compassion and understanding.

Prayer is a central aspect of the church experience, offering a direct way for individuals to connect with God and seek guidance, comfort, and strength. For Gen Zers who may face unique challenges such as academic pressure, social anxieties, and the pervasive influence of social media, prayer can be a grounding practice amidst the chaos of daily life.

Beyond personal prayer, the communal aspect of prayer within the church is equally significant. Knowing that others are praying for us can provide a deep sense of comfort and reassurance. This collective act of faith fosters a strong sense of community, where members support one another through both joys and sorrows. This tangible expression of care and concern is profoundly meaningful for a generation that often feels isolated despite being digitally connected.

Additionally, the emotional support offered by church members extends beyond prayer. Whether through counseling, mentorship, or simply being present to listen, the church provides a network of support that can help young people navigate life's challenges. This environment of mutual care and encouragement helps Gen Zers build resilience and find hope, knowing they are not alone in their journey.

A Sense of Purpose

In an era where many young people struggle to find direction and meaning, church involvement can instill a profound sense of purpose. Many in the Anxious Generation are characterized by their quest for authenticity and meaningful impact. They can find a compelling message within the church's teachings. A notable example of the hunger for purpose is evidenced by the immense and sustained popularity of Rick Warren's book *The Purpose Driven Life*.[2] With its life-changing message, this book has sold tens of millions of copies worldwide, underscoring the widespread yearning for purpose.

At church, young people are taught that they are part of a greater narrative that transcends the world's transient trends. The teachings of faith highlight that each individual has a unique role to play in God's grand design. This sense of purpose is not just a lofty ideal but is rooted in practical, everyday actions. Whether through community service, participating in missions trips, or simply being a positive influence in their immediate circles, Gen Zers are encouraged to live out their faith in tangible ways.

Moreover, the church provides numerous opportunities for young people to discover and develop their gifts and talents. Engaging in various ministries allows them to see the direct impact of their contributions. This active involvement reinforces their sense of purpose, showing them that their lives matter and can make a difference.

Encouraging church attendance can be a powerful step for parents concerned about their children's sense of direction. It connects

Gen Z with a community of like-minded individuals and grounds them in a purpose that provides clarity and motivation amidst life's uncertainties. The teachings and community of the church equip them with a framework for a life filled with meaning and intentionality.

Biblical Examples of Resilience

Attending church provides the Anxious Generation with the opportunity to learn about the resilience of biblical figures who faced immense challenges and emerged victorious. These stories of faith and perseverance offer potent lessons for young people navigating their own trials.

One of the most striking examples is the story of Joseph. Sold into slavery by his jealous brothers, Joseph endured years of hardship, including wrongful imprisonment. Despite these setbacks, he remained faithful to God and eventually became Egypt's second most powerful man. His story teaches resilience in the face of betrayal and adversity, showing that unwavering faith and integrity can lead to remarkable outcomes.

Similarly, the story of Esther highlights the courage required to stand up for one's people. As a young Jewish woman in a foreign court, Esther risked her life to save her people from genocide. Her bravery, strategic thinking, and faith in God's providence exemplify the power of resilience in the face of real and pervasive threats.

The New Testament also offers numerous examples, such as the apostle Paul, who faced relentless persecution, imprisonment, and physical suffering. Yet his letters to the early churches are filled with encouragement and steadfast faith. His resilience sustained him through his trials and strengthened the faith of countless others.

By learning about these and other biblical figures, young people understand resilience more deeply. They see that challenges and suffering are part of the human experience but can be overcome through faith, perseverance, and reliance on God. These stories provide a spiritual framework that equips Gen Z and Gen Alpha to handle their own difficulties with hope and courage.

The Anxious Generation often wonders if they are weird, if their struggles define them as an aberration or, even worse, as outcasts in society. These biblical characters remind them that they are neither weird nor alone.

Countering the Message of Social Media

In an age where social media often dictates perceptions of worth, beauty, and success, church attendance can offer a powerful counter message that speaks to the true essence of identity and value. For the Anxious Generation, who are deeply entrenched in the digital world, this alternative narrative is not only refreshing but necessary.

Social media platforms bombard young people with curated images of perfection and highlight reels of success, fostering unrealistic expectations and often leading to feelings of inadequacy and low self-esteem. The constant comparison can be mentally and emotionally exhausting, creating pressure to conform to unattainable and superficial standards.

On the other hand, a church emphasizes intrinsic worth and the inherent value of every individual from God's perspective, regardless of their online presence or popularity. The message of being fearfully and wonderfully made, as expressed in Psalm 139, affirms that each person is unique and cherished by God. This framework can provide a solid foundation of self-worth that doesn't depend on likes, comments, or followers.

Church teachings promote authenticity and vulnerability, encouraging young people to be genuine in God's eyes. In a world where digital personas often overshadow real-life identities, the church offers a space where individuals can connect on a deeper level, free from the filters and facades of social media.

The church community can provide positive reinforcement and support, countering the often critical and judgmental nature of online interactions. This environment of acceptance and love helps Gen Z navigate the complexities of their digital lives with a grounded sense of who they really are.

For parents, guiding their children to engage with the church can offer a powerful antidote to the often-detrimental messages of social media. It helps anchor their identity in something far more enduring and meaningful.

Providing Direction for Further Help

The data I noted earlier are sobering. Many young people struggle with anxiety, depression, and other mental health issues. Indeed, that's the reason we call them the Anxious Generation. While attending church offers spiritual support and community, it also plays a crucial role in providing direction for further help. Churches are uniquely positioned to guide Gen Zers toward the resources they need to navigate their mental health challenges effectively.

Many churches have established networks with mental health professionals, counselors, and therapists who share their values and understand the importance of integrating faith into the healing process. By attending church, young people can be connected with these trusted professionals who can offer specialized care and support tailored to their needs.

Counseling is another significant resource within the church. Some churches have trained leaders who can offer initial support and guidance, helping young people understand their issues from a faith-based perspective. Churches can provide a listening ear, practical advice, and spiritual encouragement while pointing people toward additional professional help when needed.

In times of crisis, churches also act as a safety net, offering immediate support and intervention. The safety net includes prayer, spiritual guidance, and connecting individuals with emergency mental health services. The church's role in providing direction for further help ensures that Gen Z does not have to face their struggles alone and can access the resources necessary for their journey toward healing.

Gen Z Will Attend if Their Parents Attend

The influence of parents on their children's spiritual habits cannot be overstated. Studies consistently show that children and adolescents are significantly more likely to attend church if their parents attend regularly. This influence varies, depending on whether it is the father, the mother, or both parents who attend church. The data supporting these findings highlight the profound impact of a parent's example on the faith development of their children.

Research from various studies indicates that when both parents attend church regularly, there is a strong likelihood that their children will follow suit. An older study by the Swiss government, often referenced in discussions about family faith practices, is still relevant today.

The study found that when both parents are regular churchgoers, about 33 percent of their children will attend church regularly as adults and about 41 percent will attend irregularly. This means that a staggering 74 percent of children will continue to have church involvement if both parents set the example.[3]

Fathers play a crucial role in this dynamic. The same study revealed that if the father attends church regularly while the mother does not, the likelihood of children attending church remains surprisingly high. About 44 percent of children will attend regularly, and 22 percent will attend irregularly. In other words, if the father attends church and the mother does not, 66 percent of children will still have some level of church involvement.[4] The father's influence is particularly significant in shaping the religious habits of children and adolescents.

On the other hand, if only the mother attends church regularly, the impact is notably less pronounced. In such cases, only about 3 percent of children will attend church regularly, with 33 percent attending irregularly, a total of 36 percent.[5] This data underscores a father's unique role in spiritual leadership within the family. It also highlights the challenges mothers face when trying to instill church-going habits in their children without the support of the father.

These findings are consistent with other research conducted in different cultural contexts. For instance, a study by the Barna Group found that a strong male role model in religious practice significantly boosts the likelihood of children adopting similar habits.[6] The study suggests that fathers who actively participate in their faith create a model of religious commitment that children find compelling and worthy of emulation.

Further supporting this thesis, the Pew Research Center found that 88 percent of teens with parents who attend religious services regularly also report attending services at the same frequency.[7]

The Institute for Family Studies also indicates that children who regularly engage in a faith community experience numerous benefits, including reduced likelihood of risky behaviors and improved overall well-being.[8] This reinforces the idea that active parental involvement in church encourages religious practice and contributes positively to children's development.

The data unequivocally shows that children and adolescents are significantly more likely to attend church if their parents, especially both parents, are regular attenders. Fathers, in particular, hold a substantial influence in this regard. This information underscores the vital role of parental involvement in the spiritual formation of the Anxious Generation, specifically church attendance, and the enduring impact of their example.

If you are a nonchurchgoing parent with Gen Zers who do not attend church, I hope this information is sufficiently persuasive to encourage you and your children to attend church. The benefits are massive.

To be clear, I have not yet addressed the most important issue, a personal relationship with Jesus Christ and the eternal implications of that relationship. I will underscore this issue later in the book. It is too important to ignore.

For now, consider the compelling reasons why we need to encourage the Anxious Generation to attend church. Ironically, the secular world also affirms the value of churches. In fact, many secular writers tell us that society needs churches to step up. We will examine that issue in the next chapter.

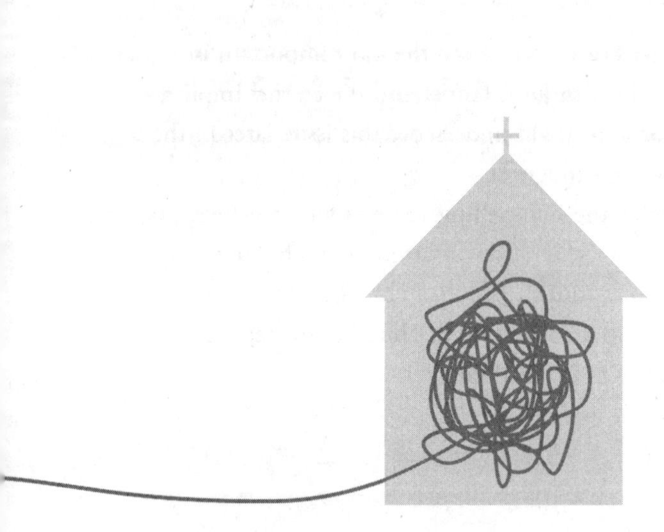

6

WHEN THE CULTURE ASKS THE CHURCH FOR HELP

IN THE 1980S AND 1990S, I served as pastor of four different churches. In each of those churches, I led a team to develop a "prospect list" that included people in our community who were not members of a church. We had different processes to follow up and contact the prospects.

Some of the prospects were Christians who had moved from another city. Some were people who had visited our church and given us their contact information. And a number of them were names we had gleaned from events our church had hosted.

Our typical method was to contact them by letter or, later, by email. Sometimes we called them. If they expressed an interest, we would visit them in person.

I remember when one of our deacons declared that we were running out of prospects. That was a first for me! The reality was that we were no longer being intentional about reaching our community. We had become dependent on waiting for people to show up at one of our worship services.

In the church where Nellie Jo and I are members and our son Jess is the pastor, we have the same closing to our worship service every week. We don't call it a benediction, but that's what it is.

Matthew 9:36-38 is shown on the screen in the worship center. Together we recite the words aloud:

> When he [Jesus] saw the crowds, he had compassion on them because they were confused and helpless, like sheep without a shepherd. He said to his disciples, "The harvest is great, but the workers are few. So pray to the Lord who is in charge of the harvest; ask him to send more workers into his fields."

This passage serves as a reminder that we will never "run out of prospects." The challenge for the church is not that there is no one left to reach. Rather, our challenge is finding sufficient numbers of workers to go into the fields to reach them. As I noted earlier, too many churches are not focused on reaching those in the harvest fields.

This culture of reaching into the community applies directly to reaching and helping the Anxious Generation. We must adopt the attitude of Jesus and have compassion for them. It is ironic that the culture outside the church recognizes this great need often with greater awareness than the church itself.

The Historical Influence of Churches on Society

Churches played a pivotal role in shaping American society, contributing immensely to various aspects of community life and national development. From the establishment of educational institutions to spearheading key movements such as the abolition of slavery, churches have historically been at the forefront of societal advancement.

My purpose in this historical excursion is twofold. First, I contend that the historical role of churches in America has made our nation stronger morally, spiritually, and socially. Second, a number of secularists today, most of whom are atheists, see significant value in churches in society. Some are even specifically asking churches to note the needs of culture and respond as we have historically.

Education

One of the earliest and most valuable contributions of churches in American society was in the field of education. Many of the country's first schools and universities were founded by religious groups aiming to educate both clergy and laypeople.

Harvard University was founded by Puritans in 1636 to train ministers. Similarly, Yale, Brown, and Princeton were established with the mission of providing religious education. These institutions grew to become prestigious centers of learning, contributing substantially to the intellectual and cultural development of the nation.

Abolition of Slavery

Churches and religious leaders were instrumental in the abolitionist movement, advocating for the end of slavery in the United States. Prominent figures such as Harriet Beecher Stowe, author of *Uncle Tom's Cabin*, and Frederick Douglass, a former slave and ordained minister, used religious arguments to highlight the immorality of slavery and mobilize public opinion against it. The Second Great Awakening, a Protestant revival movement, also played a crucial role in galvanizing anti-slavery sentiments across the nation.

Civil Rights Movement

Churches were central to the civil rights movement of the 1950s and 1960s, providing a base for organization and advocacy. Leaders such as Martin Luther King Jr., a Baptist minister, drew upon Christian teachings to promote nonviolent resistance and equality.

Churches served as meeting places for activists and as platforms for spreading the message of civil rights. Organizations founded by King and other ministers played a key role in coordinating civil rights activities and campaigns.

Volunteerism

Churches have long promoted a culture of volunteerism, encouraging their members to engage in acts of service and charity. This tradition has led to strong civic engagement and the development of numerous volunteer-based organizations. The sense of compassion, community, and moral responsibility fostered by churches became a driving force behind many social initiatives and charitable endeavors.[1]

Youth Development Programs

Many churches, both historically and today, offer programs specifically designed for youth, including educational programs, mentorship, and recreational activities. These programs provide young people with positive role models and opportunities for personal growth. By participating in church-led youth programs, young people develop essential life skills, moral values, and a sense of community. For the Anxious Generation, the need could not be more urgent.

Founding Hospitals

The establishment of hospitals by religious groups was another noteworthy contribution of churches to American society. Many of the earliest hospitals in the United States were founded by churches and religious orders to provide medical care to the needy.

Institutions such as St. Jude Children's Research Hospital and numerous other hospitals named after saints or religious figures were established with a mission to serve the sick and the poor, regardless of their ability to pay. Denominational hospitals, such as Baptist, Presbyterian, and Methodist institutions, were major contributors to medical advancements in the United States.

Disaster Relief

Churches have often led disaster relief efforts, mobilizing resources and volunteers to aid in recovery following natural disasters. One of the largest relief organizations in the world is Send Relief, a collaborative ministry of the North American Mission Board and the International Mission Board of the Southern Baptist Convention. Organizations such as the United Methodist Committee on Relief (UMCOR) and Catholic Relief Services (CRS) play crucial roles in providing immediate and long-term assistance. Their involvement ensures that affected communities receive necessary support, including food, shelter, medical care, and rebuilding assistance.

Charitable Giving

Churches have historically been centers for charitable giving, organizing support for local and international causes. This tradition of philanthropy has had a lasting impact on social welfare and humanitarian initiatives. Religious congregations collect and distribute funds to support various endeavors, including poverty alleviation, education, health care, and disaster relief.

Many Christian organizations and churches still do tremendous works of compassion today. But a pattern emerged as churches and denominations founded these institutions. Many churches and their members viewed giving to the organizations as the sum and substance of their ministry beyond the walls of the church. While funding is critical, it can be done to the neglect of action. In other words, we can end up subcontracting missions to others instead of doing it ourselves.

Meeting the needs of the Anxious Generation is largely local, focused on compassion for individuals in a church's immediate community. Such efforts certainly need funding, but they need action more. Church members must take a giving and sacrificial posture to connect with the Anxious Generation.

The Culture Asks, "Where Are You, Church?"

Yes, churches collectively have done good for society for most of America's existence as a nation. While these congregational initiatives seem to have waned over the past few decades, churches have nonetheless been a positive influence for most of the nation's history.

We are now at the crossroads of several trends that will determine whether the church is ready to respond. Unfortunately, most of these trends are not good ones.

Church attendance continues to decline. Those who have no particular belief system, the Nones, now account for about one-third of our population, though the percentage seems to have stabilized.[2] Thousands of churches close every year in America. By our estimates, the numbers range from 7,000 to 10,000 closings annually.

The number of converts to Christianity has declined precipitously over the past fifty years. That's not a surprise since only about 5 percent of churches today are intentional about reaching people with the gospel of Jesus Christ. If American churches don't start reaching more people outside of our faith, we will soon be a religious footnote in history.

I could continue with several more lamentations about the state of the American church, but you get the point. Of some 375,000 congregations, about eight out of ten are struggling to maintain the same number of attenders each year.[3] Very few churches are growing.

As churches get weaker, the need for help only gets greater. As Jesus reminds us in Matthew 9:37, "The harvest is great, but the workers are few." For the purpose of this book, the harvest is the Anxious Generation. The workers are the rest of us in the American church.

There is little doubt that the Anxious Generation is in great need. Will we have "compassion on them because they [are] confused and helpless, like sheep without a shepherd"?[4]

We hear a growing plea from the non-Christian culture for help from the religious community. Granted, these cultural cries are not necessarily to Christians specifically. They tend to be directed at religious communities in general. Still, we who account for the greatest number among these faith systems should be at the forefront of reaching out with compassion to the Anxious Generation.

Here is the irony: The non-Christian culture increasingly recognizes that churches and Christians are desperately needed. Sadly, the urgency articulated by our culture seems greater than the urgency of most churches in America.

Before we look at specific ways that Christians can help the younger generations, let's look at some examples of cultural pleas for those of us in religious communities to get our collective act together.

Jonathan Haidt

I have benefited greatly from Jonathan Haidt's book *The Anxious Generation*. Indeed, his work brought into focus many of the issues we've discussed here. Haidt calls himself an atheist, someone who doesn't believe in the existence of God. He was raised in a secular Jewish family and began identifying as an atheist around the age of fifteen. Despite his profession of "no faith," he shows a deep appreciation for the role of religion in society and often explores how religious practices contribute to community and moral development.[5]

In chapter 8 of *The Anxious Generation*, Haidt explores the psychological and societal benefits of spiritual practices, delving into their impact on individuals and communities. One of the central themes in Haidt's analysis is drawn from Pascal's concept of "the God-shaped hole," a metaphor describing the intrinsic human need for spiritual fulfillment and connection.[6]

Haidt argues that spiritual practices, including those rooted in organized religion, play a crucial role in addressing this hole. He suggests that humans have an inherent longing for meaning, purpose, and belonging—needs that are often met through spiritual engagement. This engagement can take many forms, including prayer, meditation, corporate worship, and rituals, all of which contribute to a sense of connection to something greater than oneself. The church clearly is able to fill this void.

One of the key benefits Haidt identifies is the sense of community and social support that spiritual practices foster. Religious communities provide networks of support, offering emotional and social connections. This sense of belonging and mutual support can significantly enhance mental well-being, reducing the feelings of loneliness and isolation so prevalent today. Haidt points out that communal activities, such as attending church services or participating in religious festivals, create opportunities for social interaction and bonding.

Haidt also highlights the role of spiritual practices in fostering resilience and coping mechanisms. Individuals who engage in regular spiritual practices are often better equipped to handle life's stresses and challenges. Practices such as prayer and meditation create a state of calm and a framework for understanding and accepting life's difficulties. This spiritual resilience is rooted in belief in a higher power or a greater plan, offering comfort and a sense of control in the face of uncertainty.

Another significant aspect of Haidt's perspective is the moral and ethical guidance provided by spiritual teachings. Religious and spiritual frameworks often encompass a set of values and principles that guide behavior and decision-making. These moral guidelines can promote positive social behavior, encouraging acts of kindness, compassion, and altruism.

Count Haidt among the many outside the world of Christianity who see the church as a resource to help the hurting world of the Anxious Generation. Though he does not single out the local church as the best path for these younger people, he doesn't exclude the church either.

Alain de Botton

Alain de Botton, a well-known atheist and philosopher, sparked considerable interest with his unconventional take on religion. His work in general, and particularly his 2012 book, *Religion for Atheists*, explores how the structures and practices of religion can be beneficial even for those who do not subscribe to religious beliefs.

De Botton acknowledges that religions, including Christianity, provide a wealth of valuable practices and community structures that can enrich the lives of nonbelievers. He does argue, however, that these same elements can be appreciated and utilized without accepting the supernatural claims.[7]

One of the key areas de Botton highlights is the power of ritual and ceremony. In *Religion for Atheists*, he explores how these structured practices can create a sense of continuity, order, and connection among individuals. For instance, the corporate act of attending a church service, singing hymns, or participating in religious activities fosters a sense of belonging and shared identity.

Furthermore, de Botton emphasizes the importance of the moral teachings and ethical frameworks found within religious traditions. He notes that religions have spent centuries refining principles that encourage compassion, empathy, and social responsibility. These teachings, he argues, can be valuable to everyone, regardless of their belief in a deity.

Community support is another crucial aspect of religious life that de Botton believes can benefit secular individuals. Churches often serve as hubs of social interaction and mutual aid, offering support networks for those in need.

It is clear that de Botton is yet another voice that sees the benefits of religion without it explicitly being Christianity. Can churches today capture those same benefits for the Anxious Generation without compromising the truth of the gospel to which we adhere?

Richard Dawkins

Richard Dawkins, a prominent atheist and evolutionary biologist, has long been a vocal critic of religion—and Christianity in particular. His book *The God Delusion* challenges the rationality and necessity of religious belief. However, despite his staunch atheism, Dawkins has also acknowledged the social and cultural value that religious institutions can offer.

Known for his rigorous scientific approach and sharp critiques of religious dogma, Dawkins admits that religious institutions often fulfill vital social functions. For instance, he recognizes that churches serve as community hubs where people can find social support, companionship, and a sense of belonging. In an era marked by increasing social isolation and fragmentation, the role of churches in fostering community cannot be overlooked. They offer a gathering place where individuals can form meaningful connections and support networks, which are crucial for mental and emotional well-being.

Dawkins has also expressed appreciation for the charitable work often undertaken by religious organizations. Churches frequently spearhead initiatives to help the less fortunate, providing food, shelter, and other forms of assistance to those in need. Though he argues that such humanitarian efforts do not necessitate a belief in God, he acknowledges that religious motivation can drive significant positive action. The altruistic impulse, which many find rooted in their faith, contributes to societal welfare in tangible ways.

Further, Dawkins acknowledges the role of religion in offering moral and ethical guidance. While advocating for a secular basis for morality, he concedes that religious teachings have historically provided frameworks that promote healthy social behavior. The moral principles found in religious doctrines, such as compassion, justice, and forgiveness, have helped shape ethical standards that many adhere to, regardless of their religious beliefs. These teachings can encourage individuals to act with kindness and integrity.

The cultural and historical significance of religious traditions is another aspect that Dawkins respects. He recognizes that religious stories, rituals, and symbols are deeply embedded in human culture and have influenced art, literature, music, and societal norms. This rich cultural heritage, though not requiring belief in the supernatural, is a testament to the enduring impact of religion on human civilization.

In a 2024 surprise revelation, Dawkins called himself a "cultural Christian." Of course, there is an eternity of difference between a cultural Christian and a believing Christian. Still, Dawkins is yet another secularist who sees the immense value in churches. He says, "I would not be happy if we lost all our cathedrals and our beautiful parish churches. So I count myself a cultural Christian."[8]

Sam Harris

Sam Harris, a prominent atheist and neuroscientist, has made significant contributions to the discourse on religion and spirituality.

Known for his critical stance on organized religion, Harris nonetheless recognizes and articulates the value that certain religious practices can hold. He says that secular individuals can find meaningful practices traditionally rooted in religious contexts.

Harris's work, especially his book *Waking Up: A Guide to Spirituality Without Religion*, explores the benefits of spiritual practices such as meditation and mindfulness.[9] He argues that these practices, though often associated with religious traditions, have profound psychological and neurological benefits that are accessible to everyone, regardless of their beliefs. They have been shown to reduce stress, improve focus, and enhance overall well-being.

Furthermore, Harris emphasizes the importance of community and shared experiences, which are often facilitated by religious gatherings. He acknowledges that religious communities offer a sense of belonging and mutual support that can be deeply beneficial. These communities provide a network where individuals can find emotional and social support, something that is increasingly valuable in our fragmented modern society. Harris suggests that secular organizations can learn from these religious models to create similar support structures that foster community and connection.

Harris also delves into the ethical teachings found in many religious traditions, recognizing their role in promoting positive social behavior. While he argues for a rational, secular foundation for ethics, he doesn't dismiss the moral framework offered by religions, such as compassion, empathy, and justice.

In his exploration of spirituality, Harris highlights the aesthetic and emotional experiences often associated with religious practices. He acknowledges that ritual, music, and art within a religious context can evoke a sense of awe and wonder.

Barbara Ehrenreich

Barbara Ehrenreich, a renowned journalist and social critic, offers a perspective on religion and spirituality that is read by both believers and nonbelievers. Indeed, hers is one of the cultural cries that affirms the need for churches specifically. Despite identifying as an atheist, Ehrenreich appreciates the communal and ritualistic aspects of religion, recognizing their significant contributions to human well-being and social cohesion.

In her book *Living with a Wild God*, Ehrenreich recounts her own mystical experiences, approaching them with both skepticism and curiosity.[10] Though she maintains her atheistic stance, she doesn't dismiss the profound impact these experiences had on her sense of self and her understanding of the world.

One of Ehrenreich's key insights is the role of religious rituals and ceremonies in creating a sense of order and meaning in our lives. She argues that these structured practices offer comfort and stability, especially during times of crisis or transition. Rituals such as weddings, funerals, and corporate worship provide a framework for expressing and managing our emotions, helping us navigate the complexities of life.

Ehrenreich also emphasizes the importance of community and mutual support often found in religious congregations. She recognizes that churches serve as vital social networks where people can find companionship, support, and a sense of belonging. In an increasingly individualistic society, these communal bonds are essential for mental and emotional health.

She acknowledges that religious principles such as compassion, justice, and empathy play a crucial role in guiding ethical behavior. We can only hope our nation will have sufficient healthy churches to match the great need in culture.

Elon Musk

Add Elon Musk to the choir of secular voices that affirm many of the values of Christianity. Musk has discussed his views on Christianity in several interviews, most notably during a conversation with Jordan Peterson.[11]

Musk described himself as "culturally Christian," a term he uses to express his respect for the moral and ethical teachings of Christianity, even though he doesn't consider himself particularly religious. He mentioned that he believes that the teachings of Jesus, such as forgiveness and treating others as you would want to be treated, are wise and contribute to the greatest happiness for humanity.

Musk's identification as a cultural Christian aligns with others, like Richard Dawkins, who have also used the term to describe their appreciation for Christian values and traditions, despite not adhering to the supernatural beliefs of Christianity.

Going to Church Alone

The examples here represent just a few of the pleas from the secular world for churches and religion to step up. My point is simple. Culture often sees a greater value in religion in general and churches in particular than many churchgoing Christians do. In different ways, these secularists are asking churches to look beyond themselves to a society that is lonely and hurting. Sadly, many churches have turned inward, even as the culture pleads for them to look outward.

Robert Putnam's classic critique of American culture, *Bowling Alone*, unearths massive amounts of data to demonstrate how Americans have become disconnected from one another.[12] Instead of bowling in leagues (metaphorically), we are increasingly bowling alone. Though by no means limiting his observations to religious issues, Putnam observes the incredible benefit of churches to society, particularly in how congregations reach beyond their own walls to the benefit of the surrounding culture.

To say Putnam sees the value of churches would be a vast understatement. For example, he writes, "Faith communities in which people worship together are arguably the single most important repository of social capital in America."[13] Churches, Putnam argues, provide the emotional support and connections desperately needed by culture. "Bowling alone" is an apt metaphor. In many ways, bowling alone is not really bowling at all.

Today, many Christians argue that the church is not the building but the people of God. They contend that gathering or attending is unimportant at best or legalistic. Of course, the biblical church is not wood, bricks, or mortar. But the building is the most common place where the church gathers. When we try to go it alone, we are not really the church.

Indeed, when we go to church alone (metaphorically), we are not a gathered body of believers ready to reach out and show compassion to the world beyond the church walls. We are certainly not prepared or even desiring to help the Anxious Generation.

Can we who are included in these churches change? Can we change substantively and with conviction? Can we put ourselves last and put others first? Can we, like the first church in first-century Jerusalem, be a place where we are "enjoying the goodwill of all the people"?[14]

Can we reach the Anxious Generation?

We can indeed. But first we must understand the antidote to how this generation's brains have been "rewired."

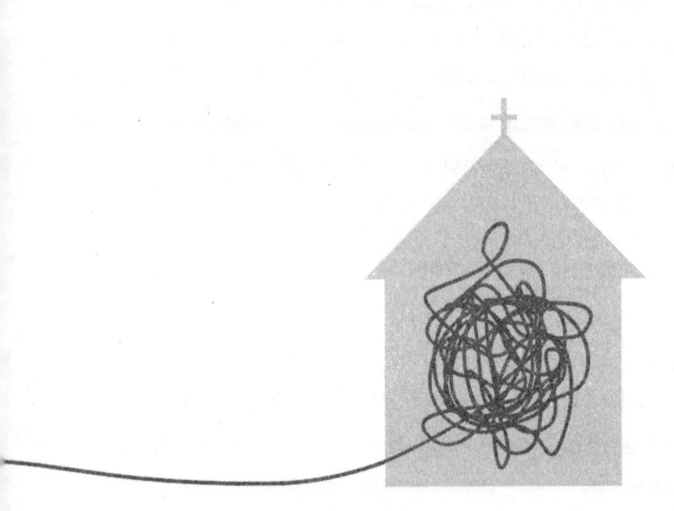

7

THE ANTIDOTE TO ANXIETY

"GARBAGE IN, GARBAGE OUT."

I remember when Dr. Martell, my professor in a corporate finance course, introduced that concept when we were studying financial projections. If you start with bad data, you'll get erroneous results. You might have the perfect formula, but it will do you no good if you don't have good input data to run.

That same principle works for our minds. If we put negative or untrue thoughts into our minds, the output will be negative results.

Garbage in. Garbage out.

Not all anxiety, depression, and negative emotion is the result of focusing on the wrong things, but much of it is. If we are told by our parents during our childhood that we are worthless, that we can't do anything, or that we are unworthy of their love, that garbage input might affect us for the rest of our lives. We may overcome it with better input, but we never forget it. For many people, self-image is a daily battle. Garbage in becomes garbage out.

To some extent, the younger generations have become the Anxious Generation because of what has gone into their minds. Of course, much of what goes into their minds is from their regular viewing and scrolling on their smartphones. With 24/7 access to social media, the Anxious Generation has become accustomed to a fictional ideal persona that they feel they must emulate. And though it's fiction, it's a very real issue for Gen Z.

So, what can be done to counteract the effects of the great rewiring? Haidt suggests several strategies. First, awareness is crucial. Understanding how social media affects mental health and behavior is the first step toward mitigating its impact. Education systems can play a role by incorporating digital literacy into the curriculum, teaching young people how to critically evaluate the information they encounter online.

Second, fostering real-life connections is essential. Encouraging activities that promote face-to-face interactions, such as sports, arts, and community service, can help counterbalance the effects of social media. These activities not only improve mental health but also build social skills and empathy.

Finally, regulating social media use is important. Setting boundaries around screen time, such as designated tech-free times or zones, can help create a healthier balance. Parents and educators can lead by example, demonstrating healthy technology habits and encouraging open discussions about the challenges and benefits of digital life.

The great rewiring described by Jonathan Haidt is a profound challenge of our time. It will require a concerted effort from individuals, families, schools, and society as a whole to address its effects.

Of course, our particular interest is seeing that same concerted effort from churches. Though there are exceptions, American churches are woefully lacking in their efforts to reach and help this younger generation. Even worse, many church leaders and church members are not even aware of the nature of the problem.

Garbage Out, Goodness In

So what does the church have to offer? As it happens, quite a lot. If garbage in leads to garbage out, it stands to reason that *goodness* in will lead to goodness out. And because God is the epitome of goodness, it seems that the church—his people on earth—might hold the antidote that will set the Anxious Generation free. In essence, it involves replacing the garbage in the minds of the Anxious Generation with the goodness of the mind of Christ. As the apostle Paul writes in Romans 12:2, "Don't copy the behavior and customs of this world, but let God transform you into a new person by changing the way you think. Then you will learn to know God's will for you, which is good and pleasing and perfect."

Goodness in, goodness out.

Paul's letter to the Philippians is amazingly prescient and incredibly relevant to the issues of today. I believe with conviction that the Holy Spirit inspired Paul to write every word.

Let's look at Philippians 4:4-8 in the context of the challenges the Anxious Generation face today:

> Always be full of joy in the Lord. I say it again—rejoice! Let everyone see that you are considerate in all you do. Remember, the Lord is coming soon.
>
> Don't worry about anything; instead, pray about everything. Tell God what you need, and thank him for all he has done. Then you will experience God's peace, which exceeds anything we can understand. His peace will guard your hearts and minds as you live in Christ Jesus.

> And now, dear brothers and sisters, one final thing. Fix your thoughts on what is true, and honorable, and right, and pure, and lovely, and admirable. Think about things that are excellent and worthy of praise.

In a world where negative thoughts and harmful comparisons dominate young minds, Paul's admonition to "fix your thoughts on what is true, and honorable, and right, and pure, and lovely, and admirable" provides a road map to mental wellness.

The Power of a New Focus

One of the key issues confronting today's youth is the constant bombardment of negative and often false information through social media. This relentless exposure to curated images and idealized lifestyles can lead to feelings of inadequacy and anxiety. Paul's directive to focus on what is true and honorable offers a powerful countermeasure. By actively choosing to dwell on positive and uplifting thoughts, young people can begin to rewire their brains away from negativity.

Paul's emphasis on thinking about what is true contrasts starkly with the deceptive nature in much social media content. Truth provides a foundation for mental stability. When young people focus on the truth of their God-given worth, their unique gifts, and the love that surrounds them, they can combat the lies that lead to anxiety and depression.

Honorable, Right, Pure, and Lovely

Paul's call to think about what is honorable and right directs the mind toward integrity and justice. In a world where ethical compromises are often glamorized, focusing on honorable actions can inspire young people to lead lives of integrity. This shift in focus can reduce the cognitive dissonance that arises when our actions don't align with our values, thereby promoting mental peace.

By encouraging thoughts that are pure and lovely, Paul directs the focus toward beauty and moral purity. In the chaos and moral ambiguity of the digital age, focusing on purity can help young people find clarity and peace. The appreciation of God's beauty that can be seen everywhere provides a respite from the negativity that often pervades social media, leading to a more serene mental state.

Admirable, Excellent, and Praiseworthy

Paul's exhortation to think about what is admirable, excellent, and praiseworthy encourages the recognition and celebration of goodness and excellence in the world. This positive focus can foster gratitude and optimism, which are crucial for mental health. By dwelling on what is commendable, young people can cultivate a mindset of appreciation rather than comparison, thereby significantly reducing anxiety.

Paul's words in Philippians 4:8 provide timeless wisdom that addresses the very core of the Anxious Generation's struggles. By fixing their thoughts on what is true, honorable, right, pure, lovely, admirable, excellent, and praiseworthy, young people can begin the process of transforming their minds. This shift in focus can help them move away from the negative influences that dominate their digital lives and toward a healthier, more positive mental state.

As we consider the implications of Paul's teachings for the modern world, it becomes clear that the ancient wisdom of the Scriptures holds profound relevance for today's challenges. The church has a unique opportunity to guide the Anxious Generation toward mental wellness by embracing and teaching these timeless principles. We can help foster a generation that is not only less anxious but also more grounded in the truth and beauty that God has provided for us.

Of course, it's one thing to say that the Anxious Generation should set its mind on these things. But it's something else entirely to put it into practice.

As we've discussed, the health of most churches in America isn't great. But even the less healthy churches among us have much to offer people, including the Anxious Generation. If God could use the church at Corinth in the first century, he can use struggling congregations today.

A Call to Worship

The Anxious Generation, immersed in a sea of digital distractions and social media pressures, often finds itself adrift without a firm anchor. One powerful antidote to this pervasive anxiety is the simple yet profound act of attending a worship service. Churches, with their unique blend of community, tradition, and spiritual nourishment, offer a sanctuary where the Anxious Generation can find peace, purpose, and a renewed sense of identity.

Worship services provide a consistent focus and a sense of belonging. In a world where digital interactions often feel superficial and fleeting, the weekly face-to-face fellowship in most church communities offers young people genuine relationships. These relationships are not based on likes or followers but on shared faith and experience.

Regular worship attendance fosters a deep sense of community, where individuals are known, valued, and supported. This sense of belonging is crucial for the Anxious Generation, many of whom desperately need a stable network of support that can alleviate feelings of isolation and loneliness.

Church worship services also introduce a different rhythm and structure from the frenetic pace of modern life. The structured nature of worship—through song, prayer, Scripture reading, and preaching—offers a point of focus away from the digital world. The regular practice of setting aside time for worship can be incredibly grounding. It allows the Anxious Generation to step away from the constant barrage of notifications and updates and to focus instead on spiritual nourishment and rest.

Moreover, worship services anchor individuals in a larger narrative. In a worship service, young people have a connection to something greater than themselves. For the Anxious Generation, often overwhelmed by the uncertainties of the future, knowing they are part of a larger plan can provide a sense of stability and hope. The message of God's love, grace, and purpose resonates deeply, offering a counternarrative to the often harsh and critical voices encountered online.

In addition, church worship services can encourage a different lifestyle. The regular exposure to biblical teaching and the example of mature Christians can inspire young people to pursue lives marked by love, integrity, and service. This moral guidance is a stark contrast to the often ambiguous values promoted by popular culture. By attending church, the Anxious Generation can be equipped with a biblical framework for life, which can reduce anxiety and increase a sense of control over their lives.

Finally, there is undeniable power in collective worship and praise. Singing praise songs and hymns, participating in prayers, and hearing the collective voices of fellow believers can be a deeply moving experience. This act of worship not only glorifies God but also reinforces the bonds of community and shared faith. For the Anxious Generation, these moments of worship can be uplifting and empowering, reminding them that they are not alone in their struggles and that they are part of a supportive and loving community.

Church worship services indeed offer a refuge for the Anxious Generation. They can play a pivotal role in alleviating anxiety and promoting mental well-being. As young people navigate the complexities of modern life, the church stands as a beacon of hope and stability, inviting them to find peace and purpose in the presence of God and the fellowship of believers.

Yes, the church is that important. Yes, the church can offer much to younger people through corporate worship. Yes, the act of consistent worship can renew and refresh their minds.

Finding Community in Groups

The Anxious Generation can often find support within the various groups that churches offer. Connecting to different groups in a church—whether they are small groups, Sunday school classes, peer groups, or ministry-based groups—provides a lifeline to young people seeking deeper connections and meaningful engagement.

Small groups—also called community groups, life groups, home groups, and other names—play an essential role in fostering community and supportive environments. These gatherings, whether held in homes, other casual settings, or church classrooms, allow for genuine relationships to flourish.

For the Anxious Generation, small groups offer a space where they can share their struggles and joys openly, knowing they are in a safe environment. These groups are built on trust and mutual support, providing a sense of belonging that is often missing in their day-to-day interactions. The intimacy of small groups helps individuals feel seen and heard, counteracting the feelings of isolation that can contribute to anxiety.

Groups of peers are another crucial aspect of church life that can significantly benefit the Anxious Generation. Youth groups, college ministries, and young adult gatherings create opportunities for individuals to connect with others in similar life stages. These peer groups offer not only companionship but also understanding and relatability.

Sharing experiences with peers who face similar challenges creates a bond that is both comforting and encouraging. These groups often engage in activities that foster community and build lasting friendships, offering a counterbalance to the often superficial connections found on social media.

Ministry-based groups provide avenues for young people to engage in service and leadership within the church. These groups focus on specific areas of ministry, such as music, outreach, missions, or children's ministry. Participation in these groups allows the Anxious Generation to discover and use their gifts and talents in service to others.

This involvement fosters a sense of purpose and fulfillment, as young people see the tangible effect of their contributions. Serving in ministry not only builds confidence and self-esteem, but it also helps shift the focus from their anxieties to the needs of others, promoting a healthier, outward-looking perspective.

In a world where young people are often left to face their anxieties alone, the church offers a caring community. By engaging with small groups, Sunday school classes, peer groups, and ministry-based groups, the Anxious Generation can find the support and connection they desperately need. These groups offer companionship and opportunities for growth, service, and deeper faith.

Reading and Studying the Bible in Church

Reading the Bible helps ground young people in God's timeless truths. The stories and teachings found within the pages of Scripture provide a foundation of stability and reassurance. When life feels like it's spinning out of control, the consistent and unwavering message of God's love, grace, and faithfulness offers a solid rock to stand on. This sense of stability is crucial for members of the Anxious Generation, who often feel as if they're navigating a sea of uncertainty and doubt.

Studying the Bible in a church setting takes this experience to a deeper level. It's one thing to read Scripture on your own, but delving into it with a community adds layers of understanding. Young people learn they're not alone in their struggles and questions. They see firsthand how others interpret and apply God's Word to their lives, offering new perspectives and insights.

The teachings of the Bible offer practical guidance for daily living. Scriptures such as Psalm 23, which speaks of God as a shepherd leading us through dark valleys, or Philippians 4:6-7, which encourages us not to be anxious but to present our requests to God, provide direct encouragement and strategies for coping with anxiety. These verses become tools for managing stress and finding peace.

Additionally, the community aspect of studying the Bible fosters a sense of accountability and growth. Young people are encouraged not only to read the Bible but also to live out its teachings. This practice helps them realign their lives with positive values and principles, promoting a sense of purpose and direction. It's about moving from mere survival to living with intention and hope.

In a world that constantly bombards the Anxious Generation with messages of inadequacy and fear, the Bible stands as an anchor of encouragement and truth. Reading and studying God's Word in the supportive context of a church community can transform people's lives. For young people searching for meaning and stability, the Bible is an invaluable resource, lighting the way through the darkest of times.

Is Your Church Ready for the Anxious Generation?

Let's see where we are at this point. First, the evidence is more than ample. Many Gen Zers are hurting, anxious, and depressed.

The level of these maladies has increased with Gen Z more than any other generation. Second, although smartphones and social media were not the only factors affecting this younger generation, they undoubtedly were major contributors. Third, the majority of the Anxious Generation would like to connect with a church. Fourth, churches can be messy and messed up and still offer hope for this younger generation. Fifth, when the Anxious Generation does come to church, they have hope of being renewed, refreshed, and transformed.

I gave three major examples of where this transformation typically takes place: in worship services, in small groups, and in ministry service. Of course, that's not an exhaustive list, but any of these three can have a positive and profound effect on young people. The combination of the three is potent.

The question that remains is this: Are churches ready and willing to reach and minister to this hurting generation?

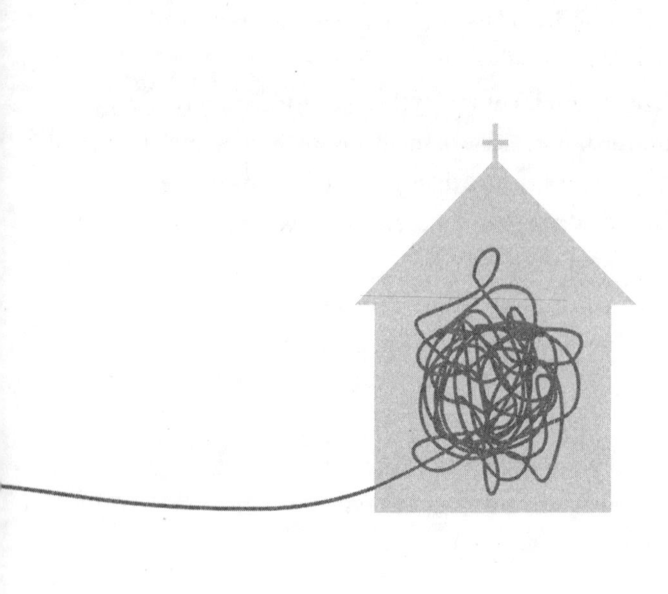

8

WHY CHURCH ATTENDANCE MATTERS

MY SON JESS AND I WERE IN THE STANDS watching our favorite football team. The stadium was packed, and the roar of the crowd was deafening. Our team had one of the best defenses in the nation. Our offense wasn't bad, but it was the defense that received most of the accolades.

Not this time. We still won the game, but only because the offense put up an uncharacteristic number of points and simply outscored the opposition. As Jess summed it up on the way to the car, "The defense didn't show up today."

Of course he was speaking figuratively. Our team had eleven players on the field when the other team had the ball, but it wasn't the stellar defense we had seen all season.

Sometimes the church doesn't show up.

I mean that literally, not figuratively.

Church members are attending church less frequently. Some are not attending at all. As we saw in chapter 3, median worship attendance of churches in the US has declined from 137 in 2000 to 50 in 2025. Those numbers are pretty sad. Though the membership of those churches declined as well, average weekly attendance decreased the most dramatically.

The church is not showing up.

We who are churchgoing Christians cannot expect to reach Gen Z, or any unchurched persons for that matter, if we are not committed to attending church ourselves. What does it say to the unchurched world when we demonstrate through our apathy that the church is unimportant? Why would the Anxious Generation want to attend a church where many of the Christians are AWOL?

Is Attendance Really That Important?

It has become common for many Christians to rationalize that church attendance is really not that important. The downward trend began in the early 2000s—long before COVID-19—but it was exacerbated by the pandemic. Because most churches switched to online worship services during the lockdown, millions of church members concluded they could do just fine without worrying about attendance.[1]

Imagine a husband and wife, married for twenty years, who decide that instead of coming home at night and spending time together, they will just FaceTime or Zoom call each other for an hour. Absurd, right? It's one thing if they travel for work and that's the only way they can stay connected while apart, but as an ongoing practice? It's a recipe for disaster.

The same is true of the church. It is absurd to treat the church with a lackadaisical attitude. If we begin to rationalize why attendance is optional, in effect we have decided that the church is unimportant. And let's be honest: An online "connection" is no real connection at all. (If it can't be avoided, sure. But there is no substitute for an embodied worship experience with other believers.)

Rationalization and Excuses

It is sadly fascinating to find church members offering a litany of excuses for why they don't attend church. The fact that they feel compelled to rationalize betrays an internal struggle. In other words, they likely know that church attendance is important, but they want to justify their absences. Here are some of the more common excuses I've heard.

"The church is the people, not the building." This one is popular because it states a biblical truth, but it uses that truth to rationalize a lack of commitment. Indeed, the people of God *are* the church, not the bricks, mortar, concrete, and wood of the building. This excuse twists a biblical truth to somehow suggest that the people of God should not gather or attend. All churches have times of gathering, and they must gather somewhere. That place is usually a building. We shouldn't be using biblical truth to justify unbiblical disobedience.

"Life is just too busy. Our schedules don't allow us to attend church regularly." The simple truth is that we prioritize what is important to us. The things we believe matter will make it onto our calendars. If church is important to us, we will attend every week, barring

sickness or disability. (And yes, I am a strong proponent of church attendance even on the road. Gathering with other faithful believers is always time I cherish.) I was on the phone recently with a friend whose church attendance had begun to wane a couple years earlier. At the time of the call, he had not been to church in more than a year. When I encouraged him to get back to being active in church and to lead his family there as well, he told me that their schedule was just too busy. He and his wife have seven children, so they are undoubtedly busy. With perhaps a bit of a sly motive, I asked him how his golf game was going. He told me it had improved dramatically since he committed to playing eighteen holes twice a week. Then he paused as the irony of his comment sank in. I wish he could have seen the smile on my face.

"It is legalistic to expect members to attend church every week." This excuse doesn't work either. You can argue that any expectation of commitment is legalism, but we don't see it that way in other parts of our lives. My grandson Nathaniel is playing high school football. I heard him telling his parents that he could not miss a practice. The coach told the team that their commitment would be demonstrated through their faithfulness in attending practice five days a week—even in the preseason heat of summer. Nobody said a word about legalism. If we're committed to something, we show up.

"The church is full of hypocrites." Yes, Christians can be hypocrites. Sometimes our actions and words don't match our beliefs. But that doesn't excuse our failure to be obedient through faithful church attendance. Is it not hypocritical to say you're a Christian who doesn't go to church?

To return to the metaphor of a marriage commitment, has there ever been a marriage where either the husband or the wife was perfect? Of course not! An imperfect spouse is not an excuse for an uncommitted marriage. Part of growing together in marriage is helping each other improve. Of course, an abusive spouse is a different story. And the same could be said of an abusive church—which I will address in the next paragraph.

"I've been hurt in the church." To be clear, there is real hurt in far too many churches. And there is no excuse for it. Abuse of any kind has no place anywhere—whether in the church or the home. I want to be careful with my words because church hurt is real in some churches. And it is my prayer that any church member who has been hurt will find a healthy church where they can recover and thrive. But having been hurt by a church is not a good reason to avoid all attendance. There are far more healthy churches than unhealthy churches, and a healthy church is a place you want to be.

"I disagree with the beliefs of the church." Most of these excuses relate to issues of secondary or tertiary doctrine. For example, someone may not affirm infant baptism. If that is a make-or-break issue, believers can find another church more closely aligned with their beliefs. Doctrinal disagreements are not a good excuse to stop attending church altogether.

"The church is irrelevant today." This statement could have many nuances of meaning. Is the church irrelevant doctrinally? Socially? Culturally? What aspect of the church do you find irrelevant? Our team at Church Answers conducted a research project to compare perceptions of church between those who attend church and those who don't. We were surprised to discover that the unchurched have a higher view of churches than many who attend church, at least on the subject of relevance.

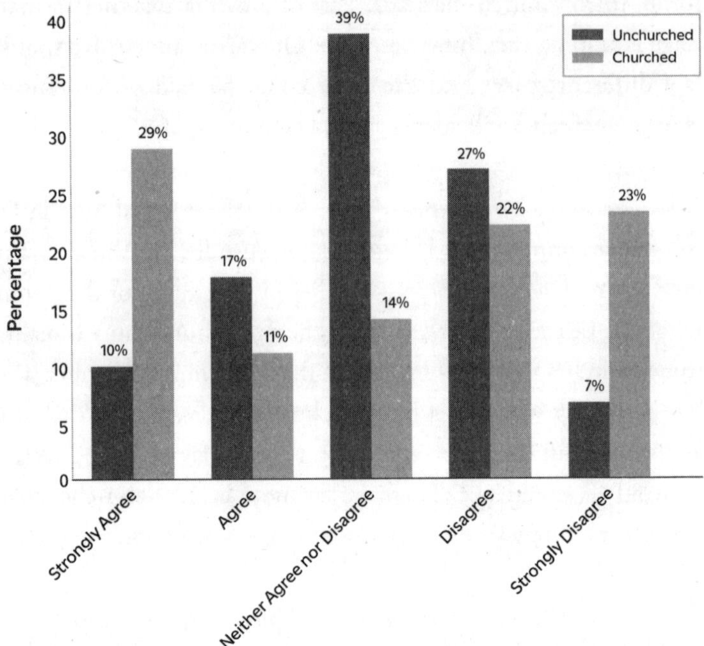

Source: New Surprising Insights from the Unchurched, Church Answers Research, 2024.

Our research indicates that only 27 percent (strongly agree + agree) of the unchurched deem churches irrelevant, while 40 percent (strongly agree + agree) of the churched have a negative view of the church's relevance.

Though we did not ask follow-up questions to discern the gap in perceptions, we are confident in our anecdotal information. Many church members find excuses not to attend church, and irrelevance is one of many.

"I don't like the style of music." This comment reflects the "worship wars" that began in the 1980s. Frankly, the battle over worship

styles reflects the consumer mindset that is evident in many churches, where church has become a matter of preference rather than commitment. I will expand on that theme in the next chapter. Still, using this excuse not to attend *any* church is absurd. There are countless worship styles available in different churches. It's simply not a legitimate reason not to attend church.

"I don't like the pastor." From the perspective of some church members, the pastor must be omnipotent, omniscient, omnipresent, and omnicompetent. But only God himself can check all those boxes. It is unreasonable and self-centered to suggest that a pastor must be able to do anything, be everywhere, and know everything.

In the past month, I heard from two different pastors who were dealing with disgruntled church members with the same complaint: They didn't visit the church members when they were at the hospital for minor outpatient surgery. In both cases, the pastors were unaware of the surgeries until the next day. One of the church members said that the pastor "should have known anyway." I think that one fits in the omniscience category.

Our conclusion? There are a lot of bad excuses among church members who attend church less frequently or drop out completely. We see the evidence repeatedly in our research and consultations. Many churches and their members are moving toward lower levels of commitment.

Why the Unchurched Say They Don't Attend Church

Our research asked the unchurched why they don't attend church. Again, the results were intriguing.

REASONS THE UNCHURCHED DON'T ATTEND CHURCH

Why do you not attend church? Choose up to three answers.

I don't believe church is necessary.	37 percent
Got out of the habit.	33 percent
I have different beliefs.	32 percent
I am not a person of faith.	26 percent
Bad experience in a previous church.	16 percent
Too busy.	15 percent
I moved to a new community.	11 percent
I don't feel welcome.	11 percent
I would not know anyone there.	11 percent
Other	8 percent
Activities of children.	7 percent
No one has invited me.	5 percent
Divorce or major family situation.	5 percent
Poor health.	4 percent

Source: New Surprising Insights from the Unchurched, Church Answers Research, 2024.

The top two answers point to a level of indifference. Non-attenders view church as unnecessary, or they simply got out of the habit of going. The third reason is predictable. A portion of non-attenders have beliefs that differ from Christianity. However, the fourth reason returns to the theme of indifference—this time, to issues of faith.

Notice the lower percentages for a previous bad church experience (16 percent), busyness (15 percent), or not feeling welcome (11 percent). What some may believe are hurdles are not that much of an issue. The unchurched don't think they are too busy, and they're not antagonistic toward the church. Issues such as divorce (5 percent) or poor health (4 percent) hardly registered on the survey.

Declining Commitment = Declining Attendance

Church Answers Research discovered several years ago that the number one reason for attendance decline was the waning commitment among church members themselves. As a simple example, a church with one hundred members who attend every week will have one hundred people in attendance. But if the members change their habits to attend only two weeks out of four, the weekly attendance will drop to fifty. In other words, a church can retain all its members and still have a precipitous decline in attendance.

A typical church loses thirty-two in attendance for every one hundred attenders in a year. Look at the breakdown:

TYPICAL WORSHIP ATTENDANCE LOST IN A YEAR (PER 100 IN ATTENDANCE)

Attendance frequency decline	15
Moving out of the community	9
Transfer to another local church	7
Death	1
Total	**32**

Source: Church Answers Research, 2024.

Sam Rainer has been at the forefront of this research for more than a decade. In 2019, he noted that less frequent attendance is a symptom of waning commitment and a precursor to even less commitment.[2] It is a vicious cycle that usually worsens over time.

If we love Christ's church, we will show up. Faithful church attendance should be a marker of committed Christianity. If we have a lackadaisical attitude toward attendance, we should never expect unchurched people, like many of the Anxious Generation, to be interested in our churches and the Good News we have to offer.

Simply stated, the church is too important to minimize. Your church attendance is a crucial marker of your faithfulness.

Why the Church Is So Important: A New Testament Perspective

From a New Testament perspective, the church stands alongside the family as one of the two institutions of great importance emphasized by Jesus. In the Gospels, he underscores the significance of both entities, each serving a unique role in the life of believers. If we truly understand how important the church is in the Bible, we cannot argue that attendance is unimportant or optional.

While the family is the foundational unit of society, the church is a spiritual family that provides its members community, instruction, and support. If we understand this as church members, we will be eager to connect with the younger generation. We will desire for them to attend church with us.

The church is often described in familial terms in the New Testament, emphasizing its role as a spiritual family. In Ephesians 2:19, Paul writes, "You Gentiles are no longer strangers and foreigners. You are citizens along with all of God's holy people. You are members of God's family."

This imagery underscores the idea that believers are not isolated individuals; they are part of a larger family where they find a sense of belonging and mutual support. This community is vital for spiritual growth and resilience, providing a network of relationships that encourage and uplift others. This community is where we should strive to invite the Anxious Generation.

Another powerful metaphor used to describe the church is the body of Christ. In 1 Corinthians 12:27, Paul states, "All of you together are Christ's body, and each of you is a part of it." This metaphor highlights the interconnectedness of believers and the diversity of gifts within the church. Each member has a unique role to play, contributing to the health and mission of the church. This interconnectedness fosters unity and cooperation as believers work together to serve God and one another.

For a generation looking for a meaningful purpose, the New Testament is clear: Gen Z will find that meaning once they become followers of Christ. They will belong to something bigger than themselves. They will not be alone.

The New Testament also emphasizes the church as a place of worship and instruction. Hebrews 10:25 urges believers, "Let us not neglect our meeting together, as some people do, but encourage one another, especially now that the day of [Christ's] return is drawing near."

Regularly gathering with other believers for worship, prayer, Communion, and the teaching of God's Word is essential for spiritual growth. The early church, as described in Acts 2:42, "devoted themselves to the apostles' teaching, and to fellowship, and to sharing in meals (including the Lord's Supper), and to prayer."

It is inconceivable that devoted followers of Jesus in the early days of the church ever saw attendance as optional. It is likewise unthinkable today that a lukewarm commitment to the church will attract the Anxious Generation.

The Great Commission, given by Jesus in Matthew 28:19-20, calls the church to make disciples of all nations. This mission underscores the church's role in spreading the gospel and serving as a beacon of hope and love in the world.

The New Testament churches were deeply engaged in outreach and service, caring for the poor, healing the sick, and proclaiming the good news of Jesus Christ. This outward focus is a critical aspect of the church's identity and purpose, calling believers to live out their faith in tangible ways.

In addition to worship and mission, the church provides

spiritual accountability and opportunities for growth. James 5:16 encourages us as believers, "Confess your sins to each other and pray for each other so that you may be healed." This practice of mutual accountability helps us stay on the path to grow in our faith. The church offers a supportive environment where individuals can be challenged and encouraged to deepen their relationship with God.

It is clear, then, that the New Testament presents the local church as an indispensable institution in the life of a Christian. A spiritual family provides belonging and support, a body where each member plays a crucial role, a place of worship and instruction, a vehicle for mission and outreach, and a community for spiritual accountability and growth.

From Acts 2 to Revelation 3, the New Testament is written in the context of the local church, explicitly addressed to local congregations and their leaders. As I often say, the church is God's plan A for reaching the world, and he did not give us a plan B.

Frankly, if church members cannot get past the issue of basic attendance, we should not expect an unchurched generation to join us.

Start Attending and Stop Apologizing for the Church

Entire church strategies to reach people have been built around timidity. We want to ensure we don't offend people as we speak the truth in love. But the cross is naturally offensive. Salvation through Christ alone is narrow thinking. Speaking of Christ's shed blood is not the most inviting conversation.

We certainly don't want to offend people simply for the sake of being offensive. We don't want to say or do stupid things. But too many church members tiptoe around matters related to their faith. They don't invite people to church because they don't want people to think they are weird. They don't begin gospel conversations because they are convinced that the person listening to them will be offended. They will typically talk about things that excite them, like their sports teams, their children and grandchildren, and their latest hobby. But not their church and their Savior. We've misunderstood the word *apologetics*—meaning a systematic discourse in defense of an idea or doctrine—to mean we should apologize for our faith (in the sense of being sorry or remorseful).

A few years ago, I attended an art workshop in another state with my wife. Though I have zero art skills, I love to see the smile on Nellie Jo's face when she is painting or conversing with other artists. This particular workshop was five days long, so we had the opportunity to get to know the others in attendance.

I knew the instructor, and I knew she was a Christian. All of the artists in the workshop were women, and three of us husbands tagged along. If I recall correctly, there were seven artists accompanied by three spouses.

The instructor asked all ten of us to come to an orientation meeting, and she opened by saying, "I'm going to ask all of you to refrain from talking about politics or religion. We don't want to offend anyone."

I caught Nellie Jo's eye. I knew we were on the same page. Why would a Christian ask other Christians to be silent? Nellie Jo and I committed to praying for opportunities to speak about our faith without being rude to the instructor. God answered those prayers repeatedly. Through unexpected questions and conversations initiated by the other artists, we were able to share our faith throughout the week.

Why are so many Christians fearful of speaking about their faith? Why do many Christians think sporadic church attendance is normal and acceptable? Why do we often apologize for our beliefs and our churches?

There is a generation that needs bold and committed Christian churchgoers to speak into their lives. As we will see, most members of Gen Z would like to go to church with you.

But they can't go to church with you if you're not there.

9

BECOMING A CHURCH WITH THE ATTITUDE OF JESUS

I LOVE WATCHING MY SONS AND DAUGHTERS-IN-LAW interact with their children. They are amazing moms and dads. They never fail to express their love for their children. They never fail to tell them how proud they are of them. They give them time. They give them physical affection.

Now of course any proud father is going to be biased toward his own family. But I can honestly say that they are among the best parents I've ever known. I am blessed beyond measure to know that my grandchildren are being raised in such loving and nurturing homes.

I would be remiss if I didn't mention that these same parents discipline their children appropriately. Yes, I am one of *those* grandparents—I believe that most of my grandchildren's transgressions are too minor to warrant discipline. But I know in my heart that discipline is important.

I have such vivid memories of an occasion when one of my grandsons, probably three years old at the time, began to disobey and talk back to his parents. Within a few minutes, his dad picked him up to take him to another room. My grandson knew what the other room held. As he was crying for mercy in his dad's arms, he reached out to me. Surely, Granddad would save him.

To his credit, my son did not give me a chance to intercede. My grandson was swiftly taken away.

A few minutes later, my son returned to the room without my grandson. I heard the little boy crying that he didn't want time-out. I asked my son if I could go in to be with my grandson. I should have anticipated his response.

"Absolutely not. He needs some time alone to think about his attitude."

Does the local church want to get serious about reaching and helping Gen Z and Gen Alpha and their families? Do we truly desire to be an avenue of healing for the Anxious Generation? If so, we each need to make certain our attitude as a church member is right. The Bible gives us a good description of what that attitude looks like. It's the attitude that Jesus had.

The Attitude of Jesus

When the apostle Paul sent a letter to the Philippians, he was writing to a real church in a real city at a particular moment in time. This letter is often called "the book of joy." The word *joy* appears seven times, and *rejoice* appears in six other places.[1] It's not a long letter, but Paul mentions *joy* in one form or another more than a dozen times! Do you think he's trying to tell us something?

Paul keenly desired for the Philippian church to focus on joy and to remain joyous. He knew their joy would lead to greater unity in the church and a more evangelistic focus outside the church.

He also knew that their joy would come from the right focus. For the Anxious Generation with smartphones and social media, their problem is "garbage in, garbage out." They focus on the wrong things—and often hurtful and dangerous things. It messes up their minds and steals their joy.

Paul tells the Philippians that their joy depends on their attitude, and he exhorts them to adopt the attitude of Christ:

> You must have the same attitude that Christ Jesus had.
>
> Though he was God,
> he did not think of equality with God
> as something to cling to.
> Instead, he gave up his divine privileges;
> he took the humble position of a slave
> and was born as a human being.
> When he appeared in human form,
> he humbled himself in obedience to God
> and died a criminal's death on a cross.[2]

Every time I read that passage, I am amazed at what Jesus did for us. From his place in heaven, he came to earth as a baby. He gave up all his royal and divine rights to become a slave for us. He humbled himself in order to save us. He loves us unconditionally. He took the punishment for our sins on a rugged cross as if he were a criminal. His agonizing death made the way for our forgiveness. His resurrection made the way for us to have eternal life.

Jesus states powerfully and clearly what his attitude means for us: "Whoever wants to be a leader among you must be your servant, and whoever wants to be first among you must be the slave of everyone else. For even the Son of Man came not to be served but to serve others and to give his life as a ransom for many."[3]

Here is the crux of the matter: If we really want to be the kind of church that welcomes and embraces the Anxious Generation, we must adopt the attitude of Jesus as our own. Many members of the Anxious Generation *want* to come to our churches. But we must ask ourselves: "If they come, will they see the attitude of Jesus in us?"

I'm not suggesting that we will be faultless. But if we are on the path to becoming more like Jesus, people will notice. It starts with our attitude, which can be seen most clearly in several areas of church life.

Faithfully Worshiping God with Others

An obvious first step is simply showing up. We must demonstrate our commitment to the local church by our attendance. Sadly, many church members have come to think of church attendance as optional. True commitment means we show up, with only rare exceptions.

Worship attendance should be the bedrock of our commitment to the church. But we are to do more than merely attend services. We are to worship the one true God joyfully with others.

I can't stay away from this description of the early church in Acts 2:46-47: "They worshiped together at the Temple each day, met in homes for the Lord's Supper, and shared their meals with great joy and generosity—all the while praising God and enjoying the goodwill of all the people. And each day the Lord added to their fellowship those who were being saved."

Now that's going to church!

Note that the members of this Jerusalem church worshiped together. It was vital for them to have a regular rhythm of worship both in the Temple and their homes. Also, note that their joy was contagious. As a result, they gained favor with "all the people." Of course, "the people" means those on the outside, those who were not yet a part of the church.

"The people" for us today means anyone on the outside of our churches, including a large swath of the Anxious Generation. The early church reached those on the outside, and people were saved day after day.

It is amazing what God will do with a unified and joyous church that worships together. The members of these churches are not demanding their own seats in the worship center. They aren't getting mad when songs are sung in a style that is not their preference. They're not more concerned about the length of the sermon or the order of worship than they are about the content of the message and the impact of the service in bringing glory to God. They are not a preference-driven church. They are a selfless, God-centered church.

By the way, churches with those same attitudes are reaching the Anxious Generation today.

May I suggest four steps toward creating a worshipful attitude?

First, attend every Sunday with rare exceptions.

Second, pray for your own heart and the hearts of others before you enter the worship center or sanctuary.

Third, pray as you enter the worship service and during the worship service.

Fourth, ask God to give you the heart of a worshiper instead of the heart of a judge seeking everything your way.

Just see what God will do with a humble, worshiping church.

Growing Together with Others

Many years ago, I led a research project on assimilation in churches. I wanted to find out how some churches effectively retained their congregation while others struggled to hold people. As a researcher, I had my presuppositions as we began the project. But I was more surprised than I've ever been by the results of that study.

The first part of our research was not a big surprise. We found that churches that focused on getting people involved in small groups had high assimilation rates. What amazed me, however, was the magnitude of this factor. The results were staggering.

Church members who became involved in some type of group in the church were *five times* more likely to still be involved in the church five years later than those who attended worship services only.

We rechecked the data several times and verified the research findings. We analyzed the church records and determined who had dropped out of active church participation. We did not include in the dropout category people who moved to another community, became incapacitated, or died. More than 83 percent of those in small groups were active in the churches. But only 16 percent of those who only attended worship services remained active in the church five years later.

When you get involved in a group in the church, such as a community group, life group, small group, Sunday school class, or home group, you develop relationships that bind you to the church. You minister to those in your group. You pray for those in your group. You serve those in your group. You also give significantly more to the church.

Do you see the connection? You are more likely to adopt the attitude of Jesus if you are in a group. If you keep at it, you will become the kind of church member who makes the church stronger. And you will be a part of a body of believers who look and act so much like Christ that they attract "all the people."

Simply stated, your commitment to a group in your church moves the church toward greater health. Others will see that in the church. The Anxious Generation will see it in the church.

Serving with Others

We've all heard the question: What would Jesus do?

That's not difficult to answer if you peruse the four Gospels.

For example, let's look at the example of Jesus with his disciples in Matthew 20:20-28. The scene opens with the mother of James and John, the sons of Zebedee. She kneels respectfully before Jesus and asks him for a favor.

"What is your request?" Jesus replies.

"In your Kingdom, please let my two sons sit in places of honor next to you, one on your right and the other on your left." The reactions of the other disciples and that of Jesus offer starkly contrasting perspectives.

> When the ten other disciples heard what James and John had asked, they were indignant. But Jesus called them together and said, "You know that the rulers in this world lord it over their people, and officials flaunt their authority over those under them. But among you it will be different. Whoever wants to be a leader among you must be your servant, and whoever wants to be first among you must become your slave. For even the Son of Man came not to be served but to serve others and to give his life as a ransom for many."[4]

Jesus tells us that we are to seek to put others before ourselves. We are to seek to be last.

In the same vein, Paul wrote to the church in Philippi, "Don't be selfish; don't try to impress others. Be humble, thinking of others as better than yourselves. Don't look out only for your own interests, but take an interest in others, too."[5]

Jesus made it clear.

Paul made it clear.

We are to have an attitude of selflessness.

We are to have an attitude of servanthood.

We are to put others before ourselves.

That spirit, which is contrary to the me-first spirit of the world, will get the attention of those outside the church and those who are not followers of Christ. We must understand the principle of godly humility if we are to reach the Anxious Generation.

Giving Generously

I'm amazed by how much an unseen discipline affects our attitude. When we give generously to the church, our attitude as church members dramatically improves. How do we know this? Jesus said so.

Of all of his parables in the Gospels, one-third are about money and possessions, more than any other topic he addresses.[6] So the discipline of giving must be important. Likewise, Jesus gives a lot of attention to money in his most well-known sermon, the Sermon on the Mount.

For example, right in the middle of his sermon, Jesus discusses the attitude we should have toward money and possessions. His words in Matthew 6:19-21 get to the heart of the matter: "Don't store up treasures here on earth, where moths eat them and rust destroys them, and where thieves break in and steal. Store your treasures in heaven, where moths and rust cannot destroy, and thieves do not break in and steal. Wherever your treasure is, there the desires of your heart will also be."

Don't miss that final sentence. The "desires of your heart" refers to your attitude. Those who give generously have a giving attitude, a serving attitude, and an attitude of commitment.

Jesus also says that if we don't hold our money loosely and give generously, we are in essence worshiping something else: "No one can serve two masters. For you will hate one and love the other; you will be devoted to one and despise the other. You cannot serve God and be enslaved to money."[7]

I wish you could have known my uncle Jess Keller. He became a second father to me when my dad died at a relatively young age.

When Uncle Jess died, I officiated at the funeral. Most funerals I officiate for older people are sparsely attended because the deceased has fewer peers still living. But for Uncle Jess's service the church was packed. And what happened at the funeral was even more amazing.

In my eulogy, I mentioned Jess's generosity. When I was a struggling seminary student with a wife and three young boys, Uncle Jess sent us money on five separate occasions over six years. I knew he was a man of prayer because the funds always came at critical times for our family. On one occasion, when I was a full-time student, I worked two jobs to provide for my family. It was still not enough to meet our basic needs.

One day, Nellie Jo showed me an ad in the newspaper where she could get paid to donate plasma from her blood. She told me she planned to go the next day.

My heart was broken. Though I was working almost every available hour, I still was not providing for my family. Nellie Jo did not hesitate to do what was necessary to take care of us.

Late that afternoon, a check from Uncle Jess arrived in the mail, and Nellie Jo never had to sell her plasma to keep us afloat.

I knew Uncle Jess was a man of prayer, because he could not have known the severity of our financial distress. One of the sentences in his letter said: "God convicted me in prayer to send you these funds."

But let me return to the scene that unfolded shortly after Uncle Jess's funeral. So many people wanted me to know that Jess had done something similar for them. Not only were their stories amazing, but the sheer number of people telling me their stories was incredible. I listened for well over an hour.

I also heard affirmations of his generosity to his church. He was serious about giving well beyond a tithe.

One man summed it up well: "Jess Keller was the most generous person I have ever known. And he seemed to take great joy in giving."[8]

You may have guessed—and you'd be right—that Nellie Jo and I named our third son after Uncle Jess.

Avoiding the Traps of Churchianity

It is far too common for churches to become inwardly focused over time. It is a natural tendency that can be overcome only with supernatural power through prayer and obedience to Christ. I call this inward focus *Churchianity*. See if you recognize some of these symptoms.

Church Becomes a Spectator Sport

When Churchianity takes hold, members attend occasionally, but they don't actively participate in the ministries of the church. They sit back and watch and occasionally offer their "valuable" input like an armchair quarterback watching a football game on television. They have no concept of biblical passages such as 1 Corinthians 12, where we are clearly told that we are not really a part of the church unless we are a functioning and participating member.

I've told the story before about the pastor who walked into a room where a tense business meeting was about to take place. Right before the meeting was called to order, he said to those in attendance, "Welcome, folks! Before we get started with our agenda for the evening, let's talk about the most important business of the church. Let's have a time of sharing. Please be prepared to tell the group how you have shared the gospel of Christ this past month."

Silence.

The business meeting went much more smoothly after that.

Church is not a spectator sport. It is a place where the members love each other and are involved with ministry inside and outside the walls of the church.

Church Is about Me and My Preferences

I call these types of churches "country club churches." You pay your dues and expect to get served by others. If you are unsure what a country club church looks like, here are some statements from church members that are indicative of that mentality. These are actual statements that came directly or indirectly from interviews with church members in our consultations.

> "Someone was in my pew last Sunday."
>
> "The pastor never listens to me about my recommendations for what he should preach."
>
> "I don't like the temperature in the sanctuary."
>
> "If we don't change our worship style, I'm not coming back."
>
> "Look, my friends and I give more money to the church than anyone else. If the pastor doesn't listen to me, the church might not be able to pay its bills. He needs to know who pays his salary."
>
> "The church decided to discontinue the 7:30 a.m. worship service because there weren't many people attending. Well, that's my worship service. If it's gone, I'm gone."
>
> "The pastor didn't visit my sister's mother-in-law in the hospital, even though I told him to."
>
> "They painted the worship center a hideous color. I just might stop giving."

You get the picture. Biblical Christianity is about serving, giving, and putting others first. Churchianity is me-centered. It is about getting my preferences met and being served by others.

Focusing on the Flaws of Your Church

If you are looking for a church that will meet all your preferences, you'll never find it. If you are looking for a church that will never mess up, you'll never find it. The churches in the New Testament were messy. They had a multitude of problems. They were full of hypocrites and sinners.

But God still used those churches, from the scandal-ridden church at Corinth to the joyous church at Philippi, which nevertheless had a major conflict between two members. We must stop apologizing for our churches. We must accept the reality that none of us will reach perfection this side of heaven. Messy church members create messy churches. We will never completely get our act together. But God works in our midst nonetheless.

Gen Z and their younger successors, Gen Alpha, do not expect perfect churches. The Anxious Generation doesn't expect human perfection; what they need is human acceptance. They need to find a church that genuinely cares about them, a church that is willing to forsake its own needs to meet their needs.

The Anxious Generation is a generation that is hurting. But it is gratifying that local churches can provide so much help to ease the pain and heal the hurts.

Perhaps surprisingly, a majority of unchurched Gen Zers say they want to attend a church. But they're unsettled about walking into a strange place by themselves. If you really want to change the world by connecting with this generation, you must take the initiative. And that is the subject of the next chapter.

You might be surprised at the positive responses you receive.

10

THE CHURCH GOES TO THE ANXIOUS GENERATION

WHEN MY FRIEND LIZ HEARD I was writing this book, she wanted me to tell her story, though the circumstances were deeply hurtful.

Liz loved her daughter, Deborah, intensely. But during her teenage years, Deborah ran away and went to live with a friend. The friend's mom called to let Liz know that Deborah was there. She wanted to see if it was okay for Deborah to be there.

"Yes," Liz said, thinking, *At least I know she's okay and not on the streets.*

Now it had been more than a year, and Deborah and Liz were still estranged from each other.

To be fair, I had never heard Deborah's side of the story. And frankly, to that point, I really hadn't heard *either* side of the story. All I knew was that Deborah had been gone for more than a year and her mom was hurting badly.

I asked Liz when Deborah's attitude began to deteriorate. As she began backtracking the years, I interrupted her.

"Out of curiosity," I said, "I'm wondering if her problems began around the same time she got a smartphone." I knew that Deborah was a member of the Anxious Generation.

My friend's jaw dropped. Her eyes opened wide.

"Oh, my goodness," she exclaimed. "How did you know?"

I told Liz about my research and some of the findings that had come back.

Liz then told me about the first time she became aware of her daughter's addiction.

"Before we gave her a smartphone, she would occasionally look at her social media accounts on our home computer," she said. "But after we gave her the smartphone when she was thirteen, things changed rapidly for the worse. I had never connected those dots until just now."

Liz continued with her story.

"Something happened when she was fourteen. She was kayaking and dropped her phone in the river. She totally freaked out!"

Liz took a breath. I could tell she was processing the event again in her mind.

"So Deborah borrowed a friend's phone in order to call me," she said slowly. "When I heard her voice, I thought something terrible had happened to her. When she calmed down enough to explain the situation, I was both relieved and angry. I was relieved because she wasn't hurt. But I was angry because she was so over-the-top upset about a stupid phone."

Then things got even worse. When Liz told her daughter that she couldn't afford another phone right then, Deborah went into complete meltdown mode. When she got home that day, she pleaded, screamed, and cried continuously.

"Do you know what she said?" Liz asked rhetorically. "She said her life was over without her smartphone! Can you believe that?"

"Yes. Based on what I've been reading about the effects of smartphone addiction among teens, I can believe it."

"She worked my husband and me until her dad couldn't take it anymore. He told me she was driving him crazy, so I charged a new smartphone on my credit card, even though we really couldn't afford it. It was maybe six months later that she took off and hasn't been back."

To this day, mother and daughter are still estranged. "Even though I yielded and replaced her phone quickly, she still won't speak to me," Liz lamented. "I always thought the phone was incidental to our separation, but maybe it was the reason for our problems."

Deborah in Church?

Can the local church really help someone like Deborah, a young person so addicted to her phone and social media that she experiences painful withdrawal when she is separated from her device?

Yes, the evidence presented in this book gives every indication that the church can be a place of solace, hope, and joy. There is potential for many victories if the Anxious Generation goes to church.

But here's the challenge: The Anxious Generation will likely *not* go to church unless the church first goes to the Anxious Generation.

Let's quickly review the first five findings of the research we summarized in chapter 4.[1]

Finding 1: *Unchurched does not always mean no church.* Many unchurched people have at least a distant or relational connection to a local church.

Finding 2: *The unchurched believe local churches are generally good for their communities.* Almost 60 percent affirmed this viewpoint.

Finding 3: *The unchurched struggle to connect with the churches in their communities.* In essence, church members are not connecting to the unchurched, particularly to the unchurched Anxious Generation.

Finding 4: *The unchurched believe churches are still relevant but not trustworthy.* I found this data point intriguing. The unchurched see the relevance of the church as an institution, though they don't trust individual churches.

Finding 5: *The unchurched are open to friendships through church but are intimidated to visit because they don't feel welcome.* Over half of non-attenders believe the church would be a good place to make new friends, but they are intimidated to visit a church on their own, without an invitation.

Let's put together these somewhat disparate pieces of the puzzle. We begin with a central thesis we've documented repeatedly. Many members of the Anxious Generation are hurting to the point of anxiety, depression, self-harm, and suicide.

Likewise, we've made a reasonable case that a somewhat healthy church can be a refuge and a place of hope for these young people. Note that I mention "a somewhat healthy church." Your congregation does not have to be perfect. But it cannot be toxic.

Further, our research shows that the unchurched population, including the unchurched Gen Z, has a mostly positive view of churches. Many of them would welcome the opportunity to meet new people and make friends at a church—if they're invited. They're not likely to show up on their own. Even though many members of the Anxious Generation would like to go to church, they don't want to go by themselves. Who can blame them? I don't like to go to unfamiliar places by myself either. Churches can seem mysterious and confusing to those on the outside looking in.

The Common Refrain

"We need to reach more young people" is one of the most common comments we hear from members and leaders of struggling churches. The members see with their own eyes that their congregation is dwindling and aging. It makes sense that they would see the need to attract the younger generations.

Unfortunately, the typical solutions are not helpful. Some churches look for a new pastor. Maybe the previous pastor left in frustration or was fired due to misplaced anger. Or maybe the pastor found it more convenient to retire, giving the church an opportunity to hire a younger pastor. The members mistakenly believe that a younger pastor will bring in the young people. But this approach rarely works. If the church wasn't reaching young people with the previous pastor in place, there isn't much hope that a new, younger pastor will be the answer.

The same is true with hiring a children's pastor or youth pastor. Again, if the church wasn't reaching young people before, a youth pastor won't be a silver bullet either.

Perhaps you noticed the common thread between these two approaches. The church is "hiring out" the responsibility for ministry, which is simply unbiblical. The mandate is for *all* church members to do the work of ministry to build up the church.[2]

There's a certain irony here. Younger people who are not in church generally would like to be. And most churches would like to "get younger" by reaching these young people. But the connections are not being made. Why? In most churches, there are several things missing.

The Missing Pieces

It was a sad ending to a promising church consultation. The church was located in a community that had thousands of young people. The opportunities to reach them were multifold. The church's facilities were not bad. It had no deferred maintenance, and it was moderately appealing from the curb.

Money was not a problem, either. The church had no debt, and the three staff members were compensated adequately. But the church was declining. They were not reaching the younger generation, many of whom were their neighbors.

When our team presented our initial findings, I anticipated the response would be full of hope and promise. On the contrary, there was a clear sense of disappointment, if not anger, toward our consulting team. It didn't take more than a few minutes to discern that what they really wanted us to deliver was a silver bullet.

Our recommendations about community outreach and evangelism didn't sit well with the pastor and the lay leadership team he had assembled to work with our consulting team. Most telling was the response of one of the lay elders, a key influencer in the church. Speaking of the young and unchurched families in the community, he said, "They know where we are. They could come here if they wanted to."

Though I had seen that attitude in many churches, I had rarely heard someone voice it as clearly and powerfully as that elder. The elder made it clear that this church was not one where the people would go out into the community and invite people in. They were going about their business and waiting for the community to come to them.

Sadly, I knew it would be a long wait.

Surrounded by the Harvest

Let's return for a moment to Matthew 9:36-38, mentioned previously in chapter 6. The message there is too important to minimize.

As we pick up the story, Jesus and the disciples are traveling through "all the towns and villages" (verse 35), teaching and healing countless people. Then Matthew shows us the scene through the eyes of Jesus:

> When he saw the crowds, he had compassion on them because they were confused and helpless, like sheep without a shepherd. He said to his disciples, "The harvest is great, but the workers are few. So pray to the Lord who is in charge of the harvest; ask him to send more workers into his fields."

Luke 10:1-3 is a parallel passage to Matthew 9:36-38, but Luke records an additional line that Jesus utters: "Now go, and remember that I am sending you out as lambs among wolves."[3] That additional sentence is a powerful reminder that we are to *go* into the fields. Our role as believers is not to wait for people to come to us. We are to go out, even among wolves, and invite people in.

By warning us that we are like "lambs among wolves," Jesus reminds us that evangelism is spiritual warfare, and though we are told to go, we dare not enter that world in our own power and strength. The enemy will do everything he can to hinder our work. As we go, we must pray so that our efforts will be in Christ's power.

The apostle Paul was emphatic about prayer: "Pray in the Spirit at all times and on every occasion."[4]

The Bible gives us a clear plan to reach the Anxious Generation. We are not only to *pray* for workers to go into the field. We are to *be* the workers who go into the field. We are to love the Anxious Generation and have compassion for them. We no longer have the luxury of doing church as usual, nor should we. The opportunity to reach the Anxious Generation is urgent. We can't wait for them; we must go out to them.

But what does it mean to go into the fields where the Anxious Generation is? Frankly, there is no template response or program. These younger generations, both Gen Z and Gen Alpha, are not monolithic. Like the culture at large, they vary by race, ethnicity, politics, preferences, and family structure. They are just like those of us who are in the church, except they're not in the church. And by every indicator, many of them are open, if not eager, to connect with Christians and the local church.

Even though there isn't a template, we can follow some basic guidelines as we reach out to the Anxious Generation. Different churches will contextualize their approach to reaching these young people.

Love Them

Jesus had compassion for the crowds. The Greek word translated *compassion* is rich in its meaning and implications. It generally refers to a person's inner parts, such as the heart, lungs, liver, or intestines. In the ancient world, these inner parts were considered the seat of a person's emotions, particularly empathic emotions such as pity, compassion, and love.

As Jesus ached for those who were hurting and had compassion for those who were lost, so should we for the Anxious Generation. But how do you have compassion for people you haven't met? How do you love people you might not understand—and who might not understand you? The answer is simple: *pray*. Jesus said to pray for the workers who go into the harvest fields. Likewise, the workers must pray to love those in the fields. Though our love may seem insufficient, God's love through us is never lacking. Pray individually and pray as a church that you will genuinely love these younger people. Pray that God's love will be abundant and evident in you.

Second, *learn* from the Anxious Generation. If we are willing to spend time with people who are different from us, we will begin to see the world through their eyes. As we gain their perspective, we will understand them better. As we understand them better, we will have countless opportunities to serve them and introduce them to the Savior we know and serve.

Get Uncomfortable

Please hear me clearly. Whenever a church begins to reach people who are not Christians, the church begins to change. In fact, the church usually gets downright messy! What a pity that so many church members see the church as a religious country club, where they pay their dues and expect to have their personal preferences and needs met. That attitude will not only repel the Anxious Generation, but it will also repel anyone else outside the walls of your church.

If your focus as a church member is insisting on a specific music style, being comfortable in your own pew or chair, demanding that the order of worship and sermon conform to your preferences, and reminding leadership that your contribution pays the bills and their salaries, then don't even try to reach the younger generation.

Most older church members want their church to reach younger people—that is, until those younger people begin to change and reshape the church. It simply won't work. We must be willing to be uncomfortable to reach the younger generations, especially with those who don't believe as we do.

We must have a posture of servanthood. Such a disposition is good regardless of our setting, but it is essential when we begin to reach beyond the walls of the church. Jesus reminded us that being uncomfortable and sacrificial defined his ministry, and it should likewise define our lives: "For even the Son of Man came not to be served but to serve others and to give his life as a ransom for many."[5]

Invite Them

Jesus' method of inviting people to follow him was as varied and personal as the people themselves. Throughout the Gospels, he reaches out to individuals in ways that speak uniquely to their circumstances, needs, and hearts. His invitations were not just about words; they were about actions that demonstrated his deep understanding and love of people.

In Matthew 4:18-22, Jesus called Simon Peter and his brother Andrew as they were fishing. He simply said, "Come, follow me, and I will show you how to fish for people!" Immediately, they left their nets and followed him. The simplicity of this invitation carries a profound implication: Jesus offered them a new purpose in life.

Similarly, Jesus called James and John while they were mending their nets. He didn't need a lengthy explanation or persuasion; his presence and authority were enough to compel them to leave their father and livelihood behind. These calls were personal and transformative, offering these men a direct invitation into a new life.

In Matthew 11:28, Jesus extends a compassionate invitation to those burdened by life's struggles: "Come to me, all of you who are weary and carry heavy burdens, and I will give you rest."

Here, Jesus reaches out to those who feel overwhelmed and offers them rest, not just in a physical sense, but a deep, soul-refreshing rest that only he can provide. His invitation is gentle and empathetic, acknowledging the weariness of the human condition and offering relief through his presence.

Jesus also invited those who were genuinely seeking truth and righteousness. In John 1:35-39, when John the Baptist's disciples ask Jesus where he is staying, he responds with an open invitation: "Come and see."[6] This invitation was not just about physical proximity; it was an invitation to explore and discover who Jesus was, to spend time with him and learn from him. It was an invitation to a relationship with him.

Perhaps the most powerful examples of Jesus' invitations are those extended to sinners and outcasts. In Luke 19:1-10, Jesus invites himself into the home of Zacchaeus, a despised tax collector.

"Zacchaeus! . . . Quick, come down! I must be a guest in your home today."[7] In so doing, Jesus not only invited Zacchaeus to a meal but also into a powerful encounter that led to repentance and salvation.

Similarly, in John 4, Jesus engages a Samaritan woman at the well outside of town, inviting her into a deeper understanding of who he is. He offers her "living water,"[8] which is an invitation to eternal life and a true purpose in life.

Finally, Jesus' invitation extends to all people, as seen in Matthew 22:1-14, where he tells the parable of the wedding feast. Here, the invitation to the feast symbolizes God's invitation to his Kingdom, extended to anyone willing to accept it. This invitation is inclusive, crossing social and cultural boundaries and emphasizing that everyone is welcome in God's Kingdom.

Jesus' invitations were always personal, powerful, and purposeful. Whether he was calling fishermen to become his disciples, offering rest to the weary, engaging seekers of truth, reaching out to sinners, or extending a universal call to all, Jesus knew exactly how to meet each person where they were and invite them into a life-changing relationship with him. His approach was always filled with grace and truth, reflecting his desire for every person to know him and follow him.

Though we cannot extend invitations to the Anxious Generation with the precise insights and wisdom that Jesus employed, we can certainly invite them in ways both genuine and personal. Rather than offering an oblique, "I would love for you to visit my church," we can fully engage by saying, "I would love to take you to my church and treat you to lunch afterward."

The latter invitation is personal and meaningful. It is an investment of our *presence*—of our time and attention. It invites the other person into a relationship. Simply inviting someone to visit is not really an invitation at all. It's too casual and noncommittal. And if the person were to come, the two of you might not even have an interaction. The thought of showing up at a church entirely on their own is a massive barrier to the Anxious Generation—and I'm certain they're not alone in that! It can be intimidating when you don't know what you will encounter. But if you invite someone—and maybe even pick them up or at least agree to meet out front—and then walk with them into the building, sit together, and then take them out for brunch or lunch, those barriers will come crashing down.

The potential harvest is indeed great. Are you willing to be one of the workers to go into the fields?

Reaching Out to Emma

I am the oldest person in my community group at church. Emma is the youngest. There is a gap of forty-five years between us. I love the cross-generational classes that allow an old geezer like me to interact with younger adults.

Emma is from Gen Z. She is part of the Anxious Generation. But unlike many of her peers, she is not an *anxious* member of the Anxious Generation. She is now a follower of Christ, learning how to find her identity in him.

I'm not suggesting she doesn't have challenges that can cause moments of anxiety—we all do. Indeed, she comes from a difficult home situation and has physical challenges that might discourage a lot of people. After graduating from high school, she didn't have the support of her family to further her education or find a job. She did both mostly on her own.

Emma, in many ways, is the poster child for "I can do all things through Christ, who gives me strength."[9] Though she is nearly a half-century younger than I am, I look up to her with respect and awe.

She and I interacted briefly about this book as I was writing it. Every time I said something about the Anxious Generation, Emma responded knowingly.

"Yes," she would often say, "I see that all the time."

Whenever I converse with Emma, I realize I am talking with a member of the Anxious Generation who found a church and also found Christ. In her case, the story did not begin with a member of the Anxious Generation going to church. It began when the church went to the Anxious Generation.

Emma came to our church as a teenager, when she was invited by someone who cared enough about her to accompany her. She discovered that the church offered comfort, peace, and hope that she could not find elsewhere. Even more important, she discovered Jesus and his saving power.

Today, Emma is in her twenties and growing in her relationship with Jesus and in her connection with the local church. A committed family in our church provided her with a home for a season, and they gave her transportation to church. Emma's story is an example of what can happen in the lives of the Anxious Generation when the church is willing to go outside the four walls and invite people in.

They are waiting. Many are ready to hear from you. Many are ready to connect with you.

Are you ready? Are you willing to be a part of the church that goes to the Anxious Generation?

That is the question every churchgoing Christian must answer.

11

BECOMING A CHURCH FOR THE ANXIOUS GENERATION

THE INQUIRY WAS SIMILAR to so many we receive at Church Answers. The pastor's words were both heartwarming and sad.

"I fear that our church is dying," he began. "Our members are fewer in number, and they are much older than just a few years ago. We want our church to survive, and we want to reach younger people. But more than anything, we want to love and support young people. I think we could make a difference in their lives. But there is no reason they would visit our church, much less join our church. We are just a bunch of old folks."

The pastor was right in many ways. Because the remaining members are primarily senior adults, his church will likely die unless something changes. He was also right that younger people will not visit his church unless something changes.

What I heard from that pastor, however, and subsequently saw in his church, was a heart for people. He wanted his church and ministry to make a difference. I had little doubt that he would do whatever it took to make a difference for Christ. He just didn't know where to begin.

After working with churches for more than four decades, I can attest to the desire of most to help others, particularly those in crisis. If we explain to church leaders the mental health crisis pervasive in the Anxious Generation, they will want to help.

But they need at least a framework for moving forward. Perhaps you are among them. What would it take for your church to become a church for the Anxious Generation?

Where to Begin?

Please hear me clearly. There is no template or checklist for moving forward. There is no fixed formula for reaching young people. There is no plan guaranteed to change the lives of the Anxious Generation.

But there is a starting point. It is the starting point I recommend to all churches.

Pray.

A few years ago, we introduced a ministry we called the Hope Initiative. It is not a one-size-fits-all approach. It is simply a way to get a church looking beyond its own walls to the community around them. The ministry is simple. It is built around the thirty days of challenges I outline in my book *Pray & Go*.[1] The challenges are simple, but they can become life changing.

To say we've been amazed at this ministry is a big understatement. Thousands of churches have taken these challenges, and we are grateful to God for his work in those churches.

As we continue to hear reports from churches using the Hope Initiative, we have discerned an emerging pattern. As churches begin to focus on prayer, their members start to focus more on people outside the walls of the churches than on themselves. Call it a Great Commission mindset, or an outward focus, or an evangelistic burden. It is an initial and necessary step for churches to accomplish the mission God has called them to.

It is the necessary first step to reach the Anxious Generation.

You don't have to use the Hope Initiative as your solution. Use whatever tool or ministry works best for your church. Most of the great movements of God began with a few dedicated people committed to praying. If you have a few people in your church, you have enough people. God typically starts with the few to reach the many.

The Need Is Known, But It Must Be Defined

Your church members know there are societal problems that affect their lives. They know that the struggles are pervasively present in younger generations. But they might not know why the issues are so daunting to the Anxious Generation.

Gen Z was the first generation to go through adolescence with smartphone technology and social media shaping or "rewiring" their minds, according to Jonathan Haidt. The internet was the foundation. The smartphone was the portal. And social media provided the content and aspirations. It was a dangerous combination that no previous generation had ever known.

The societal and peer pressure young people feel to have a smartphone is enormous. My sons and their wives are doing an excellent job raising my grandchildren. I wish I had demonstrated their wisdom in my own parenting years. Yet I have witnessed firsthand the disruption of family life caused by smartphones. It is not a mere fad; it is a pervasive and powerful reality. I was present when one of my grandchildren received a smartphone for his fourteenth birthday. He did not merely shout for joy; he ran laps in the house with his arms raised like he was at a Pentecostal revival meeting.

His parents are wise and exceedingly careful about how their children can use their phones. They limit viewing time. They make sure the phones have the appropriate safeguards. They don't hesitate to take the phones away if they become an obvious hindrance to school focus and good behavior.

But smartphones and the world behind them are a deep and powerful attraction. For many in Gen Z and Gen Alpha, the smartphone has become an idol in the true biblical sense of the word. It is not just a cultural malady. For many whose minds have been shaped by this force, it is a spiritual sickness. Churches must recognize this reality. We are dealing with the first of the Ten Commandments. We have idols in our midst.

Such is the reason we begin with prayer. We are dealing with forces no human power can handle. But the second step, *awareness*, follows prayer. We must bring this issue to our churches. Our members know something is wrong, but many can't define it. Few of us older people would ever have believed in the malevolent power of a device that can fit in our pockets. Not all idols are towering sculptures.

The Church of the City in the Nashville area brought the issue to the awareness of their multisite congregations with a Twenty-Eight-Day Digital Fast. Over four weeks, Pastor Darren Whitehead led the church to a clearer understanding of the potential destructive power of smartphones. Each week had a specific emphasis:

Week 1: Detach. Remove the most distracting apps and use your phone for calls and texts only.

Week 2: Discover. Find healthier activities to replace the time that was dedicated to your smartphone.

Week 3: Delight. Rediscover God's creation, meaningful conversations, and healthy activities.

Week 4: Determine. Make a few lasting changes discovered in the past four weeks.

Darren Whitehead knows that, like the Hope Initiative for prayer and evangelism, the Twenty-Eight-Day Digital Fast is not a silver bullet to solve all the maladies of the world today. However, like the Hope Initiative, it is an opportunity to address the need with a beginning-point solution.[2]

Sometimes, even a brief comment in a sermon or presentation can open eyes to the great need. I made one comment in a presentation that became the source for multiple inquiries for weeks to come. I phrased it as two questions: "Did you know that the average teenager spends 1,752 hours a year on social media through their smartphones? Can you imagine how transformative their lives would be if they used those hours instead to make a difference in the world?"[3]

If You Invite Them, They Will Come

It's not a great mystery, nor does it defy conventional wisdom. The majority of the Anxious Generation will come to your church if someone personally invites them.

In the Church Answers research project I mentioned earlier, studying comparable attitudes between churchgoers and the unchurched, we found that the unchurched have a more favorable attitude about the relevance of church than many who attend church. Unchurched people are more likely to attend church than a churched person is to invite them.[4]

Robert D. Putnam's classic book *Bowling Alone: The Collapse and Revival of American Community* examines the decline of social capital in America since the 1950s.[5] Through extensive research, Putnam demonstrates that Americans have become increasingly disconnected from family, friends, neighbors, and democratic structures. He explores how traditional forms of civic engagement—such as joining clubs, attending public meetings, and participating in community organizations like the church—have steadily declined, leading to a society with weaker social bonds and reduced trust.

Putnam's book was written seven years before the introduction of the first smartphone, and a decade or more before the convergence of smartphones, the internet, and social media apps. But his points have only been magnified as people have become more disconnected than ever from one another.

The Anxious Generation abandoned real community to make time for its counterfeit. That statement is both foreboding and hopeful. The loss of community is ominous. However, the opportunity for the church to become that community is promising.

Remember, the majority of the Anxious Generation say they would go to church if invited. If they come to church, they will discover community. As they discover community, some of the adverse effects of the great rewiring of their brains can be reversed.

However, invitations to the Anxious Generation must be personal rather than a mass-produced marketing program. Invite individuals personally. Accompany them to church personally. Develop a relationship with them personally.

In chapter 4, I wrote about using the tool Invite Your One to help churches create a culture of invitation.[6] The most frequent comment we receive through this ministry is something like this: "I was shocked at how easy it is to invite someone, and I was shocked that she responded positively to my invitation."

Churches can positively tap into the younger generations' deep desire for community. Indeed, our data indicate that churches might be at an inflection point to see an upsurge in positive responses to invitations to discover community in the church.

Simply stated, millions of Anxious Generation members would love to receive an invitation to church. The simple act of inviting them will become a journey of transformation for those who discover the community available in the local church.

The opportunities for churches that take this step are boundless. The harvest is indeed great, and we can be among the "more workers" that God sends into his fields.[7] Go out into your community and invite them in. If you invite them, they will come. When they come, they will hear the greatest news ever about a Savior who has compassion on them and loves them unconditionally.

Prepare for Things to Get Messy

Church is already messy. If we do what God is calling us to do, it will get even messier. To be clear, that's not a reason not to do it. But be prepared for what God will do in your midst—and *how* he may choose to do it. Perhaps more than any previous generations, today's young people will bring a lot of baggage and mental health issues. How will your church respond to issues that you may not have seen before? How will your congregation react to the anxiety, the mental health issues, and the abundance of new questions?

The first admonition is simple: *Love them.* Have compassion on them. Pray with them and for them.

The second admonition is to *proceed with caution.* That doesn't mean *hold back.* It's simply a word to the wise. Most churches and church members are not equipped to deal with anxiety, depression, and other mental health issues. Indeed, it's possible our attempts to help may do more harm than good. We advise churches to be prepared to refer those suffering emotional and mental health issues to qualified Christian professionals. You need a plan for what to do when the problems are too big. But that isn't to suggest that every member of the Anxious Generation will walk through your doors with seemingly insurmountable problems. Indeed, most will respond well to love, care, and community.

Creating a mental health triage plan for church members involves establishing clear guidelines for when to provide counseling within the church, when to refer individuals to outside help, and how to identify situations that require emergency action. Here's a general framework that can guide these decisions.

When to Offer Counseling Within the Church

Spiritual or faith-based issues. When struggles are primarily spiritual (such as dealing with doubt, grief, or seeking purpose), church staff or pastoral counseling may be well-suited to help.

Mild emotional challenges. If someone is dealing with life stressors (such as relationship issues, minor anxiety, or sadness) and appears stable, church counselors can often provide guidance, prayer, and support.

Behavioral support in community. For those who would benefit from ongoing accountability and encouragement within the church community, offering church counseling or support groups may be ideal. Indeed, the church should strive to get everyone into some type of regularly meeting group.

When to Recommend Outside Help

Moderate to severe mental health issues. Diagnosed conditions such as chronic depression, significant anxiety disorders, or trauma-related issues often require specialized, professional mental health support. Develop a list of referrals.

Complex issues beyond the church's expertise. If an individual's needs go beyond the training or experience of church counselors (such as needing cognitive-behavioral therapy or psychiatric evaluation), an external referral is best.

Signs of dependency or addiction. For issues involving substance abuse, addiction, or self-harm behaviors, recommend outside treatment to ensure the person receives comprehensive care.

Build a List of External References

Qualified mental health professionals. Compile a list of trusted counselors, therapists, psychologists, and psychiatrists who share the church's values and are sensitive to faith-based perspectives.

Affordable and accessible resources. Consider options for low-cost or sliding-scale services to ensure accessibility.

Emergency contacts. List crisis hotlines, local mental health crisis units, and emergency contacts for situations that require immediate intervention.

When to Consider the Situation an Emergency

Immediate risk of harm. If a person expresses suicidal thoughts, shows intent to harm themselves or others, or is actively in crisis, consider it an emergency. Immediate action should include contacting emergency services (911) or guiding them to the nearest hospital emergency room.

Severe psychotic symptoms. If someone is experiencing hallucinations, severe paranoia, or delusional thinking that puts them or others at risk, the situation is critical. Call 911 for medical assistance.

Acute behavioral change. A sudden, drastic change in behavior (such as severe withdrawal, aggression, or loss of touch with reality) could indicate an urgent mental health crisis.

Having a structured approach will provide clarity, support, and safety for both the church leaders and the congregation. Additionally, educating church members on mental health and promoting the use of these resources can help build a community that feels empowered to seek help as needed.

Let me add two important notes here. First, this triage plan can be implemented by any church of any size. The triage plan might seem a bit challenging at first. However, we have worked with churches with fewer than thirty in attendance that have been able to develop a triage plan.

Second, I strongly recommend Sam Rainer's book *Make My Church Safe*.[8] It covers safety issues well beyond mental health crises, and it is an excellent resource for any congregation to address a variety of considerations for safety within a congregation.

When I served as pastor of a church in Birmingham, Alabama, we were blessed to welcome a number of people who had recently become followers of Christ. After about a year of evangelistic growth, I was confronted by a long-term member who told me that our evangelistic emphasis was destroying the comfort and fellowship of "her" church. She told me pointedly, "We have too many messy people in our church who don't know anything about church etiquette." And yes, I specifically remember her using the words *church etiquette*.

Before I could respond, she looked at me sternly and asked, "What are you going to do about it?"

Perhaps my response was not entirely godly, but I replied, "I'm glad that Jesus loved messy people. I plan to pray that God will keep us reaching these messy people no matter what happens to *his* church."

Yes, I could have tempered my response. But I was glad I didn't yield to her self-centered attitude and demands. I walked away praying for my own attitude and that I would be an example to lead our congregation into the harvest fields . . . no matter how messy the process might be.

Have a Path of Discipleship in Place

A path of discipleship is a straightforward process in a church that seeks to reach people and move them toward greater maturity as followers of Christ. The path of discipleship should be visual and able to be grasped by everyone in the church. In most cases, the path will limit itself to church-centered steps of discipleship. For example, it would include a new members class or similar entry point. However, it doesn't include personal Bible study, which is done outside the church. Personal disciplines are vitally important, but they are not typically included in discipleship activities in the context of the church's ministries.

The concept of a path of discipleship began to grow with the publication of *Simple Church*, which I wrote in 2006 with coauthor Eric Geiger.[9] Its growth accelerated during the COVID-19 pandemic as church leaders had the time and space during the quarantine to think about their church's future.

I have assembled nearly one hundred paths of discipleship from as many churches. While there is a variety of expressions of it, they usually have common themes. Here is one example:

The Hope Initiative → New Members Class → Small Group → Ministry Involvement

The concept is simple. The Hope Initiative is an evangelistic outreach effort.[10] It seeks to reach those who are not Christians and those who are not attending church. Once they become followers of Christ, we encourage them to join a new members class where they will learn three major aspects of the church:

1. **Information:** What are the basic issues a new member should know about our church?
2. **Expectations:** What do we expect of all members of our church?
3. **Assimilation:** How can members get involved in the church? And why should they?

After new members go through the membership class, they should understand the church and what is expected of them as members. The action item is to get every member involved in a small group and a specific ministry in the church.

You won't find the phrase "path of discipleship" in the Bible, but the concept is nonetheless helpful. It provides clarity to the church's priorities. The church can then focus and build on its key ministries and can reduce or eliminate less-essential activities. Church leadership is able to align activities strategically with the overall mission of the church.

In recent years, our team at Church Answers has noticed that more congregations added *mentoring* to their discipleship path. Here's what an expanded discipleship path might look like:

The Hope Initiative → Mentoring → New Members Class → Small Group → Ministry Involvement

We discovered that the addition of mentoring was a response by churches that were reaching the Anxious Generation. These teens and young adults were not ready to jump into a new members class as soon as they came to the church. They needed a trustworthy guide to help them understand their faith as well as to navigate the intricacies of the local church.

Some churches had fixed periods of mentoring, anywhere from three months to a year. Other churches left it open-ended. The mentoring relationship concluded when both parties signaled that the new Christian was ready to move on to a new stage of discipleship.

If our churches are fruitful in reaching more members of the Anxious Generation, I fully expect more churches will offer the young generations a period of one-on-one mentoring. It will be a labor-intensive effort, but it really looks closer to the way Jesus called and mentored his disciples.[11]

The Challenge, the Opportunity

The Anxious Generation has lost so much. Sadly, many of them do not even realize what they have lost. Compared to earlier generations, they have lost community. So-called friends on social media are often not true friends. Gen Z has lost their identity. Many members of this generation only know who they are by how they are defined on the screens that captivate them.

Tragically, so many of this generation have lost hope. That hopelessness manifests itself in anxiety, depression, self harm, and suicide. The name Jonathan Haidt gave them is accurate. They are the Anxious Generation.

But there is another movement taking place. It is a countermovement to the dark world often experienced by Gen Z and Gen Alpha. It is a revitalizing church movement. It is defined by thousands of churches that are tired of going through the motions of playing the church game. These churches are not only tired of declining; they are tired of not making a difference in the world.

My prayer is for these two movements to meet. Even more, I pray that these two movements will collide. They are both powerful. But one offers the hope that the other lacks.

I loved discovering some admirers of the church I did not know existed. Some are agnostics. Others are atheists. Some simply describe themselves as secularists. Jonathan Haidt, the author of *The Anxious Generation*, self-identifies as an atheist who is generally nonreligious.

But regardless of how they view themselves, they tend to see the good that comes from local churches. They love the intentionality of community present in the churches. They respect the moral functions of religion in general. They admire the sacrificial lives displayed by many church members. They are sometimes in awe when they see Christians worshiping together. They desire to learn more about the unity present in many congregations, especially in today's polarized world. They know that being a part of a local church means being a part of something greater than themselves.

So these non-Christians often see churches and religion as at least a partial solution to provide hope for Gen Z and Gen Alpha.

I agree with them, at least in part.

The church can offer community—a guiding compass of morality, unity, and service. Churches can indeed offer hope.

But my agreement is not in full because there is more to the story. Allow me to conclude this book with a true story about Benjamin, a Gen Zer born in 1999. In this story, you will understand why I agree with the non-Christians "at least in part."

Benjamin is a classic example of a member of the Anxious Generation. He had the advantage of growing up in a comfortable middle-class home with two parents who loved him. He told me his family was a perfect example of the median household income. He was not wealthy, but he was rarely lacking in material needs.

For reasons you've read in this book, Benjamin suffered anxiety and depression. He contemplated suicide, but he told me he didn't believe he would ever really take his own life. In a refrain we heard many times from Gen Zers, he wondered if there was really any more to life than the life he had experienced.

When Benjamin took his first full-time job "when my parents were about to kick me out of the house," he met Darren, his supervisor, who was twenty years older than Benjamin.

Benjamin was drawn to what he saw in Darren, who was calm and reasonable, and sincerely wanted to help others.

"He seemed at peace with the world in a way I could not explain," Benjamin told us.

It didn't take long for Benjamin to discover that Darren was "religious." And it didn't take long for Darren to invite him to church and lunch afterward. Benjamin told us that he felt really weird sitting in a worship service with Darren, his wife, and their four kids that first Sunday.

Benjamin found that he really liked the church. He loved singing in the worship service. Over time, he began to somewhat understand the sermons the pastor preached. He was curious about so many things. He tried not to be a pest to Darren, but he had a ton of questions. Darren suggested they meet once a week to talk about some of his questions. Darren bought Benjamin a Bible, and that became a focal point for their meetings.

After they had met for a few months, Darren calmly encouraged Benjamin to embrace the Christ he was studying.

Two months later, Darren was taken aback when he ran into Benjamin at the coffee shop where they often met. He was startled by his friend's appearance, though he couldn't pinpoint what the difference was. Darren immediately asked Benjamin if he was okay.

Benjamin smiled.

"Darren," he began, "I know I'm a sinner. Early this morning, I prayed that Jesus would forgive my sins. I knew he would. He took the punishment for my sins by dying on a cross. He was put into a borrowed tomb, but that dead body rose from the dead. He defeated death. He defeated sin."

There was a moment of silence. To Darren, it seemed like a moment of powerful holiness.

Controlling his emotions, Benjamin spoke softly, "Darren, I have accepted the free gift of salvation Jesus gave me."

He paused again.

"I am a Christian."

The End. The Beginning.

Because Darren had been faithful to invite Benjamin to church, and to follow up with an invitation to meet on a regular basis, Benjamin found community.

He embraced the worship in the church.

He loved doing ministry in the community with church members.

He gained clarity as he learned the moral teachings of Jesus.

So those non-Christian observers are right, but only partly right. They are right that religion and local churches can help the Anxious Generation. The positive benefits of a worshiping community are real and powerful.

But the story can't end there. It must end with a beginning.

It is called the new life. It is called being born again.

True victory takes place not only when the Anxious Generation goes to church, but also when the Anxious Generation comes to Christ.

Notes

FOREWORD

1. Robert D. Putnam, *Bowling Alone: The Collapse and Revival of American Community*, rev. ed. (New York: Simon & Schuster Paperbacks, 2020), 1.
2. Warren Buffett at the 1994 Berkshire Hathaway annual meeting, Warren Buffet Archive, April 25, 1994, 1:48–1:53, https://buffett.cnbc.com/video/1994/04/25/buffett-you-dont-find-out-whos-been-swimming-naked-until-the-tide-goes-out.html.

INTRODUCTION: COMING TO GRIPS WITH THE ANXIOUS GENERATION

1. Jonathan Haidt, *The Anxious Generation: How the Great Rewiring of Childhood Is Causing an Epidemic of Mental Illness* (New York: Penguin, 2024), 4.
2. Sharon Edelin, "Gotlib Case—20 Years Later," (Louisville) *Courier-Journal*, June 2, 2003, 1A.
3. Haidt, *Anxious Generation*, 3–4.
4. Jonathan Haidt, "Overview" on website about *The Anxious Generation*, https://jonathanhaidt.com/anxious-generation.
5. Haidt, *Anxious Generation*, 9. Italics in the original.
6. Jean M. Twenge, *Generations: The Real Differences Between Gen Z, Millennials, Gen X, Boomers, and Silents—and What They Mean for America's Future* (New York: Atria Books, 2023), 28.
7. Haidt, *Anxious Generation*, 9–10.
8. Haidt, *Anxious Generation*, 6–7.
9. Haidt, *Anxious Generation*, 9.

CHAPTER 1: GENERATION GAPS

1. "Just How Many Baby Boomers Are There?," Population Reference Bureau (PRB) website, accessed November 25, 2024, https://www.prb.org/resources/just-how-many-baby-boomers-are-there.
2. Jean M. Twenge, *Generations: The Real Differences Between Gen Z, Millennials, Gen X, Boomers, and Silents—and What They Mean for America's Future* (New York: Atria Books, 2023), 345.
3. From the subtitle of Jean M. Twenge, *iGen: Why Today's Super-Connected Kids Are Growing Up Less Rebellious, More Tolerant, Less Happy—and Completely Unprepared for Adulthood* (New York: Atria Books, 2017).
4. Twenge, *Generations*, 346.
5. United States Census Bureau Household Pulse Survey; data collected August 2024 to September 2024. Cited in Jean M. Twenge, "The Surprising Number of Young Adults Who Identify as Nonbinary," *Generation Tech* Substack, accessed October 30, 2024, https://www.generationtechblog.com/p/the-surprising-number-of-young-adults.
6. Twenge, *Generations*, 350.
7. Twenge, *Generations*, 372–373.
8. Twenge, *Generations*, 374.
9. Twenge, *Generations*, 376.
10. Twenge, *Generations*, 376.
11. See "Life Births, Birth Rates, and Fertility Rates, by Race of Child: United States, 1909–80, from the Centers for Disease Control and Prevention," accessed December 17, 2024, https://www.cdc.gov/nchs/data/statab/t1x0197.pdf; "Live Births and Birth Rates, by Year," Infoplease, updated July 27, 2023, https://www.infoplease.com/us/population/live-births-and-birth-rates-year; and "US Birth Rate 1950–2024," Macrotrends, https://www.macrotrends.net/global-metrics/countries/USA/united-states/birth-rate.
12. The Internet of Things is "a network of interrelated devices that connect and exchange data with other IoT devices and the cloud. IoT devices are typically embedded with technology such as sensors and software and can include mechanical and digital machines and consumer objects. . . . With IoT, data is transferable over a network without requiring human-to-human or human-to-computer interactions. A *thing* in the internet of things can be a person with a heart monitor implant, a farm animal with a biochip transponder, an automobile that has built-in sensors to alert the driver when tire pressure is low, or any other natural or man-made object that can be assigned an [IP] address and can transfer data over a network." Source: Kinza Yasar and Alexander S. Gillis, "internet of things (IoT)," TechTarget Network, last updated June 2024, https://www.techtarget.com/iotagenda/definition/Internet-of-Things-IoT.

CHAPTER 2: FOUR THREATS TO OUR YOUNG PEOPLE

1. See "A Short History of the Internet," *Science and Media Museum*, December 3, 2020, https://www.scienceandmediamuseum.org.uk/objects-and-stories/short-history-internet.
2. See, for example, chapter 1, "The Surge of Suffering," in Jonathan Haidt, *The Anxious Generation: How the Great Rewiring of Childhood Is Causing an Epidemic of Mental Illness* (New York: Penguin, 2024).
3. US National Survey on Drug Use and Health. See also, Haidt, 24. The US National Survey on Drug Use and Heath releases data every other year on key issues affecting the mental health of youth. The data cited here comes from "Youth Ranking: Youth with At Least One Major Depressive Episode" for 2010 and 2020, noted in their section on Mental Health America.
4. US National Survey on Drug Use and Health. See also, Haidt, 27. The US National Survey on Drug Use and Heath releases data every other year on key issues affecting the mental health of youth. The data cited here comes from "Anxiety Prevalence by Age for 2010 and 2020" noted in their section on Mental Health America.
5. "Emergency Room Visits for Self-Harm," US Centers for Disease Control, National Center for Injury Prevention and Control, 2010 and 2020.
6. "Suicide Rates for US Adolescents, Ages 10–14," US Centers for Disease Control, National Center for Injury Prevention and Control, 2010 and 2020.
7. Haidt, *The Anxious Generation*, 123–125.
8. Kira E. Riehm et al., "Associations Between Time Spent Using Social Media and Internalizing and Externalizing Problems Among US Youth," *JAMA Psychiatry* 76, no. 12 (September 11, 2019): 1266–1273, https://doi.org/10.1001/jamapsychiatry.2019.2325.
9. J. W. Patchin and S. Hinduja, "2023 Cyberbullying Data," Cyberbullying Research Center, February 16, 2024, https://cyberbullying.org/2023-cyberbullying-data.
10. Alexandra Dane and Komal Bhatia, "The Social Media Diet: A Scoping Review to Investigate the Association Between Social Media, Body Image and Eating Disorders Amongst Young People," *PLOS Global Public Health* 3, no. 3 (March 22, 2023): e0001091, https://pubmed.ncbi.nlm.nih.gov/36962983.
11. Jessica C. Levenson et al., "Social Media Use Before Bed and Sleep Disturbance Among Young Adults in the United States: A Nationally Representative Study," *Sleep* 40, no. 9 (September 2017): zsx113, https://doi.org/10.1093/sleep/zsx113.
12. Mary Madden et al., "Teens, Social Media, and Privacy," Pew Research Center, May 21, 2013, https://www.pewresearch.org/internet/2013/05/21/teens-social-media-and-privacy.

CHAPTER 3: SHOULD THE ANXIOUS GENERATION GO TO CHURCH?

1. 2020 Faith Communities Today survey, Hartford Institute for Religion Research, Hartford Seminary, Hartford, Connecticut, https://faithcommunitiestoday.org/wp-content/uploads/2021/10/Faith-Communities-Today-2020-Summary-Report.pdf. The 2025 number is an estimate from Church Answers Research.
2. Acts 2:46.
3. Matthew 16:18.
4. See "The Four Ways Almost Every Growing Church Does It," *Rainer on Leadership* podcast, episode #763, August 23, 2022, where Sam Rainer and I discuss this typology of church growth. Visit https://churchanswers.com/podcasts/rainer-on-leadership/the-four-ways-almost-every-growing-church-does-it/.
5. See, for example, Ryan Burge, "What Predicts Church Growth or Decline?," *Graphs about Religion* Substack (paid subscription), March 14, 2024, https://www.graphsaboutreligion.com/p/what-predicts-church-growth-or-decline.
6. Acts 1:8.
7. These numbers are qualitative estimates. I reviewed the data from churches I consulted with during those years, which is admittedly a small sample size. Still, I'm confident that the trends are accurate even if the numbers are not precise.

CHAPTER 4: WHY THE ANXIOUS GENERATION DOESN'T GO TO CHURCH

1. Ryan Burge, "The Nones Have Hit a Ceiling," *Graphs about Religion* Substack (paid subscription), May 20, 2024, https://www.graphsaboutreligion.com/p/the-nones-have-hit-a-ceiling.
2. Burge, "The Nones Have Hit a Ceiling."
3. Ryan Burge, "We Asked the Nones a Bunch of Questions about Leaving Religion," *Graphs about Religion* Substack (paid subscription), July 15, 2024, https://www.graphsaboutreligion.com/p/we-asked-the-nones-a-bunch-of-questions.
4. *The State of Religion and Young People 2020: Relational Authority*, Springtide Research Institute, 2020.
5. "How the Unchurched Really Feel about the Churched," Church Answers Research, August 2024. The study sample was 604 people with a margin of error of +/– 4 percent at the 95 percent confidence interval. Our research didn't focus only on younger people, so the results likely reflect all age groups that have abandoned the church.
6. *How the Unchurched Really Feel about the American Church*, copyright © 2024 Church Answers and Church Answers Research, all rights reserved, https://churchanswers.com/new-surprising-insights-how-the-unchurched-really-feel-about-the-american-church/.

7. Thom S. Rainer, *The Unchurched Next Door: Understanding Faith Stages as Keys to Sharing Your Faith* (Grand Rapids, MI: Zondervan, 2003).
8. For more information, see www.InviteYourOne.com.

CHAPTER 5: WHEN THE ANXIOUS GENERATION GOES TO CHURCH

1. Thom S. Rainer and Art Rainer, *Raising Dad: What Fathers and Sons Learn from Each Other* (Nashville, TN: B&H, 2007).
2. See Rick Warren, *The Purpose Driven Life: What on Earth Am I Here For?*, expanded ed. (Grand Rapids, MI: Zondervan, 2002, 2011, 2012).
3. Robbie Low, "The Truth about Men and Church," *Touchstone* magazine, June 2003, https://www.touchstonemag.com/archives/article.php?id=16-05-024-v.
4. Low, "The Truth about Men and Church."
5. Low, "The Truth about Men and Church."
6. Barna Group, *Households of Faith: The Rituals and Relationships That Turn a Home into a Sacred Space*, Barna Research, 2019.
7. Jeff Diamant and Elizabeth Podrebarac Sciupac, "10 Key Findings about the Religious Lives of US Teens and Their Parents," Pew Research Center, September 10, 2020, https://www.pewresearch.org/short-reads/2020/09/10/10-key-findings-about-the-religious-lives-of-u-s-teens-and-their-parents/.
8. Tyler J. VanderWeele, "Religious Upbringing and Adolescence," Institute for Family Studies, September 18, 2018, https://ifstudies.org/blog/religious-upbringing-and-adolescence.

CHAPTER 6: WHEN THE CULTURE ASKS THE CHURCH FOR HELP

1. See Robert Wuthnow, *Acts of Compassion: Caring for Others and Helping Ourselves* (Princeton, NJ: Princeton University Press, 1991).
2. "About Three-in-Ten US Adults Are Now Religiously Unaffiliated," Pew Research Center, December 14, 2021, https://www.pewresearch.org/religion/2021/12/14/about-three-in-ten-u-s-adults-are-now-religiously-unaffiliated/.
3. At Church Answers, we keep track of between 700 and 1,200 churches a year through our consultations, pastoral coaching, and queries to our organization. Prior to COVID-19, 65 percent of the churches with whom we interacted had declining attendance. The number of declining churches jumped to slightly more than 80 percent during the post-pandemic years of 2021 to 2024.
4. Matthew 9:36.
5. See, for example, Haidt's books *The Righteous Mind: Why Good People Are Divided by Politics and Religion* (New York: Pantheon, 2012) and *The Happiness Hypothesis: Finding Modern Truth in Ancient Wisdom* (New York: Basic Books, 2006).

6. Jonathan Haidt, *The Anxious Generation: How the Great Rewiring of Childhood Is Causing an Epidemic of Mental Illness* (New York: Penguin, 2024), 215–216.
7. See Alain de Botton, *Religion for Atheists: A Non-Believer's Guide to the Uses of Religion* (United Kingdom: Hamish Hamilton, 2012).
8. Theo Hobson, "Is Richard Dawkins a Christian?" *The Spectator*, April 2, 2024, https://www.spectator.co.uk/article/does-richard-dawkins-know-what-he-thinks/.
9. Sam Harris, *Waking Up: A Guide to Spirituality Without Religion* (New York: Simon & Schuster, 2014).
10. Barbara Ehrenreich, *Living with a Wild God: A Nonbeliever's Search for the Truth about Everything* (New York: Twelve, 2014).
11. "I'm 'Culturally Christian,' Elon Musk Says in Interview with Jordan Peterson," *Zenit*, August 3, 2024, https://zenit.org/2024/08/03/im-culturally-christian-elon-musk-says-in-interview-with-jordan-peterson.
12. Robert D. Putnam, *Bowling Alone: The Collapse and Revival of American Community* (New York: Simon & Schuster, 2000).
13. Putnam, *Bowling Alone*, 66.
14. Acts 2:47.

CHAPTER 8: WHY CHURCH ATTENDANCE MATTERS

1. For more on this topic, see my book *Where Have All the Church Members Gone?* (Carol Stream, IL: Tyndale Momentum, 2024).
2. Sam Rainer, "How a Decrease in Attendance Frequency Is Affecting Your Church," *Sam Rainer: Leading the Established Church* (blog), November 17, 2019, https://samrainer.com/2019/11/how-a-decrease-in-attendance-frequency-is-affecting-your-church/.

CHAPTER 9: BECOMING A CHURCH WITH THE ATTITUDE OF JESUS

1. See Philippians 1:4, 18, 25; 2:17, 18, 29; 3:1; 4:1, 4.
2. Philippians 2:5-8.
3. Mark 10:43-45.
4. Matthew 20:24-28.
5. Philippians 2:3-4.
6. C. W. Bradley, "The Stewardship of Our Material Possessions," sermon, copyright 1982, 2004 by Truth for Today, http://www.biblecourses.com/English/en_lessons/EN_198211_04.pdf.
7. Matthew 6:24.
8. I previously told this story in my book *I Will: Nine Traits of the Outwardly Focused Christian* (Nashville, TN: B&H, 2015), 71–72.

CHAPTER 10: THE CHURCH GOES TO THE ANXIOUS GENERATION

1. "New Surprising Insights from the Unchurched," *Rainer on Leadership* podcast, episode 878, Church Answers Research, November 5, 2024, https://churchanswers.com/podcasts/rainer-on-leadership/new-surprising-insights-from-the-unchurched-releasing-new-research/.
2. See Ephesians 4:12.
3. Luke 10:3.
4. Ephesians 6:18.
5. Matthew 20:28.
6. John 1:39.
7. Luke 19:5.
8. John 4:10.
9. See Philippians 4:13.

CHAPTER 11: BECOMING A CHURCH FOR THE ANXIOUS GENERATION

1. Thom S. Rainer, *Pray & Go: Your Invitation to Become a Great Commission Christian* (Carol Stream, IL: Tyndale Momentum, 2023).
2. See Darren Whitehead, "The Joy of Missing Out: Lessons from a Church-Wide Digital Detox," *After Babel* Substack, October 23, 2024, https://www.afterbabel.com/p/the-joy-of-missing-out-lessons-from.
3. See Jonathan Rothwell, "Teens Spend Average of 4.8 Hours on Social Media Per Day," Gallup, October 13, 2023, https://news.gallup.com/poll/512576/teens-spend-average-hours-social-media-per-day.aspx.
4. See *How the Unchurched Really Feel about the American Church*, copyright © 2024 Church Answers and Church Answers Research. All rights reserved. https://churchanswers.com/new-surprising-insights-how-the-unchurched-really-feel-about-the-american-church/.
5. Robert D. Putnam, *Bowling Alone: The Collapse and Revival of American Community* (New York: Simon & Schuster, 2000).
6. See www.InviteYourOne.com.
7. See Matthew 9:36-38.
8. Sam Rainer, *Make My Church Safe: A Guide to the Best Practices to Protect Children and Secure Your Congregation from Harm* (Carol Stream, IL: Tyndale Momentum, 2024).
9. Thom S. Rainer and Eric Geiger, *Simple Church: Returning to God's Process for Making Disciples* (Nashville, TN: B&H Books, 2006).
10. See www.hopeinitiative.com.
11. Two classics on reaching and discipling (mentoring) people were written by Robert E. Coleman: *The Master Plan of Evangelism* (1963) and *The Master Plan of Discipleship* (1987).

About the Author

THOM S. RAINER is founder and CEO of Church Answers. With forty years of ministry experience, Thom has spent a lifetime committed to the growth and health of the local church and its leaders. Prior to founding Church Answers, Thom served as president and CEO of LifeWay Christian Resources. Before LifeWay, he served at The Southern Baptist Theological Seminary for twelve years, where he was the founding dean of the Billy Graham School of Missions, Evangelism, and Ministry. He is a graduate of the University of Alabama and earned his MDiv and PhD from The Southern Baptist Theological Seminary. In addition to speaking in hundreds of venues over the past thirty years, Thom led Rainer Group, a church and denominational consulting firm that provided church health insights to more than five hundred churches and other organizations from 1990 to 2005. Thom has authored more than forty books. He and his wife, Nellie Jo, live in Franklin, Tennessee.